Non-Knowledge and Digita

Other Titles in the Series

Digital Cultures Series

Edited by Andreas Bernard, Armin Beverungen, Irina Kaldrack,
Martina Leeker and Sascha Simons

A book series of the *Centre for Digital Cultures*

Non-Knowledge and Digital Cultures

edited by
**Andreas Bernard, Matthias Koch
and Martina Leeker**

μ **meson press**

Bibliographical Information of the
German National Library
The German National Library lists this publication in the
Deutsche Nationalbibliografie (German National Bib-
liography); detailed bibliographic information is available
online at http://dnb.d-nb.de.

Published in 2018 by meson press, Lüneburg
www.meson.press

Design concept: Torsten Köchlin, Silke Krieg
Cover image: © Lily Wittenburg
Proofreading: Janet Leyton-Grant, Selena Class
Proofreading and typesetting assistance: Inga Luchs

The print edition of this book is printed by Lightning Source,
Milton Keynes, United Kingdom.

ISBN (Print):   978-3-95796-125-9
ISBN (PDF):   978-3-95796-126-6
ISBN (EPUB):   978-3-95796-127-3
DOI: 10.14619/1259

The digital edition of this publication can be downloaded
freely at: www.meson.press.

Contents

NON-KNOWLEDGE

KNOWLEDGE

OPACITY

EPISTEMOLOGY

DIGITAL MEDIA

[1]

Introduction: Non-Knowledge and Digital Cultures

Matthias Koch

Digital media today are accompanied by emphatic stances on knowledge, non-knowledge, and their relation to one another. Generating, distributing, and making available massive amounts of data that take form by modeling, digital media provide us with abundant information and potentially new ways of gaining knowledge. This has been attracting various, sometimes radical scenarios in which technology either eliminates non-knowledge or plants it deep within contemporary cultures, due to the alleged universal power and opacity of algorithms. Both conceptualizing and researching non-knowledge have proven to be epistemological challenges that are key to understanding contemporary digital cultures.

The great number of twentieth and twenty-first century discourses on non-knowledge can, among other factors, be linked
to such diverse aspects as automatization and media historical
developments, risk management, a rise in prognostics, ecological
and social developments, or the perception of a general rise in
complexity (Wehling 2009). Non-knowledge has shown to be a
pervasive topic, be it in political and economic debates, amongst
the general public or in a huge number of academic fields. In the
latter, the twentieth century saw a strongly growing interest in
epistemology, in criticizing traditional concepts of knowledge,
in unveiling and analyzing unquestioned premises of research,
ideas of self-evidence, and blind spots. From a perspective of
contemporary history directed at the status of digital media,
the broad and often emphatic discussions of non-knowledge
may be seen as a "symptom of a fundamental uncertainty about
our mechanized life-world" (Burkhardt 2017, 57, translated by
the author). At the same time, histories and theories of non-
knowledge need to reflect on themselves as being part of a long-
standing tradition of questioning the status of knowledge—a
temporal horizon going way beyond the twentieth century, with
roots in antique skepticism or the philosophies of enlightenment.

When dealing with these debates and the problems they
articulate, a characteristic terminological diversity quickly
becomes apparent. In the English language, *non-knowledge*,
nescience, and *ignorance*, with the latter arguably being the
most common one, all concern closely related problems (for
an attempt at theoretical differentiation cf. Gross 2010, 53–56).
While these expressions each have individual etymologies and
conceptual histories, they share a semantic field and the attempt
to signify something that poses grave epistemological problems
to conceptualization. Therefore, speaking of *Non-knowledge
and Digital Cultures* neither excludes other existing terms nor
does it claim to deliver a theory exclusively tied to this expression. Rather, emphasizing the expression *non-knowledge* serves

to direct attention to "the 'natural' reverse side of knowledge"
(Gross 2016, 313), i.e. to their reciprocal relation.

Corresponding to the great diversity of thematic contexts in
which non-knowledge is being discussed, there is a huge variety
when it comes to analytically determining that which is called
non-knowledge. For example, non-knowledge can be regarded as
factual absence of knowledge, as a conscious or non-conscious
state of *not knowing something*. This notion can, for example,
be virulent in questions about the relation between the growth
of knowledge and the respective growth of non-knowledge
in science, in taking non-knowledge as a productive force,
in differentiations between unspecified and specified non-
knowledge, in assumptions about fundamentally unknowable
things ("Ignorabimus"), in a conscious or non-conscious attitude
of ignoring facts or a decision not to know something, or in
intentionally obfuscating knowledge and keeping another party
from knowing. Here, the expression *non-knowledge* stands in
for something that is not, not yet, or not supposed to be known,
that is not at all accessible, that is a result of ignoring facts or
that is concomitant with gaining knowledge. Non-knowledge in
this sense may be seen as an obstacle in need of overcoming,
as a necessity in the development of knowledge, or even as a
fundamental human right, i.e. in the case of debates on genetic
diagnostics.

One of the key epistemological aspects in these and many other
contexts is whether the relation between non-knowledge and
knowledge is modeled as an oppositional one (non-knowledge
not being knowledge) or as a complementary one (non-knowledge
being the *flipside of knowledge*). It seems more productive to
describe this relation in the latter sense: given, for example, that
the conscious or non-conscious determination of anything as
knowledge, knowable, or worthy of knowing will always entail the
exclusion of something else as non-knowledge, not knowable,
or ignorable. Also, in research, theoretical framework, selection
of sources, hypotheses, institutional factors, social contexts

and structures of power lead to both including and excluding specific questions and topics. Furthermore, only when reflecting upon this complementary relation does it become possible to acknowledge and discuss the structuring function of the non-conscious structures and regularities of cultural techniques, tacit knowing, or historical a prioris, i.e. the non-conscious ratio constitutive of individual and collective practices. In return, conceptualizing non-knowledge this way necessarily determines the assessment of research itself, a relation prominently represented by a certain understanding of media theory.

> The specific methodology of media knowledge displays itself in the insistent relation that it maintains to non-knowledge. … [It] sounds out the conditions of … rules of enunciation insofar as they cannot be perceived or are constitutively occluded. (Holl 2015, 84)

One could argue that *non-knowledge*, *ignorance*, or *nescience* —expressions rather than *termini technici*—are conceptually productive, both individually and as parts of a shared semantic field, precisely because they are logically underdetermined. In other words, the logical ambiguity and negativity of these expressions correspond to the characteristics of what they try to grasp. They are reminiscent of the way in which, drawing on Claude Lévi-Strauss, floating signifiers work. These signifiers "occur to represent an indeterminate value of signification, in itself devoid of meaning and thus susceptible of receiving any meaning at all; their sole function is to fill a gap between signifier and the signified" (Lévi-Strauss 1987, 55f.). Building on Lévi-Strauss, Ernesto Laclau speaks of empty signifiers: being universalistic and underdetermined at the same time, their function lies in stabilizing hegemonic discourses. Such a signifier represents the "theoretical possibility of something that indicates the discursive presence of its own limits from within the process of signifying" (Laclau 1996, 36). An empty signifier stands in for a structural impossibility of signifying. Laclau's critical view would serve well in discussing the political implications and biases of

non-knowledge discourses, e.g., regarding debates on Big Data, **15**
surveillance, and the right to anonymity.

Despite the differences between the aforementioned aspects of
that which is called non-knowledge, ignorance, or nescience, the
difficulties of gaining insight into it are what these expressions
have in common: all of them logically determine non-knowledge
primarily via its opacity and implicitness. In this sense, all of them
rest on the term being a signifier without a fixable signified. Given
that the term non-knowledge points to something that, logically
speaking, is a negative, conceptualizing it as a floating or empty
signifier could highlight some key difficulties in signification.

Discussing the epistemological challenges tied to non-knowledge
and its relation to knowledge is of great value to digital cultures
research. It brings up the question of whether digital technology
goes along with a qualitatively new mode of entangling knowing
and not knowing. This question currently fuels vast amounts
of research, attracting both emphatic stances on the alleged
revolutionary nature of digital technology and careful, tentative
descriptions of the historical, technological, and epistemological
conditions of knowing and not knowing today. One prominent
topos in current research is that at the core of contemporary
media culture there is a fundamental epistemic opacity (Humphreys 2009), which relates to thoughts about the unrepresentability of algorithms (Galloway 2012, 78–100) and their governmental power (Rouvroy 2011). Other key factors for this opacity
are found in the ubiquity of digital media and their deep insertion
into all sorts of everyday practices, perception, and body
techniques, leading up to a "transformation of the contemporary
affective fabrics" (Baxmann, Beyes, and Pias 2012, 9, translated
by the author). All-encompassing and altering the capacities of
sensation, such a situation has been called an ecology of affect
(Angerer 2017).

All this makes digital cultures research a prominent case of the
perceived contemporary crisis of representation, and focusing on

non-knowledge promises to deliver valuable insights into these epistemological dilemmas. It implies discussing the means, range, and limits of current scientific description and understanding. It also highlights the basic questions of what is thought of as known/not known and knowable/not knowable today, the various historical contexts of today's situation, and even the question of whether one can operationalize non-knowledge to learn about digital cultures. Relating non-knowledge to digital cultures may not only tell us something about the status of digital media as a topic of research, it may also tell us something about the status of contemporary interdisciplinary media research itself.

Acknowledgements

This volume originated from the *Non-Knowledge and Digital Cultures* symposium held in January 2016 at Leuphana University, Lüneburg, Germany. We are very thankful to the symposium participants (Timon Beyes, Paula Bialski, John Durham Peters, Eva Illouz, Noortje Marres, Claus Pias, Katja Rothe, and Christoph Wulf) for their valuable, inspiring talks, vivid discussions, and, of course, for the essays arising from the symposium.

This book itself wouldn't be the way it is if it weren't for helpful and professional aides and assistants. A big thank you goes out to Inga Luchs for her work on typesetting and formatting the manuscript, and to Janet Leyton-Grant for her patient and accurate proofreading. Moreover, we want to express our gratitude to the editorial board for cooperative and important critical reviews. Finally, we are indebted to and want to thank Ina Dubberke, Samantha Gupta, and Armin Beverungen for their support and paramount organizing talent, for both the symposium and the publication. Their commitment, and that of our Centre for Digital Cultures (CDC) colleagues, affords us the opportunity for truly transdisciplinary scholarship, discussion, and academic exchange.

References

Angerer, Marie-Luise. 2017. *Ecology of Affect: Intensive Milieus and Contingent Encounters*. Lüneburg: meson press.

Baxmann, Inge, Timon Beyes, and Claus Pias. 2012. "Ein Vorwort in 10 Thesen." In *Soziale Medien – Neue Massen*, edited by Inge Baxmann, Timon Beyes, and Claus Pias, 9–15. Zürich/Berlin: diaphanes.

Burkhardt, Marcus. 2017. "Vorüberlegungen zu einer Kritik der Algorithmen an der Grenze von Wissen und Nichtwissen." *Jahrbuch Technikphilosophie*: 55–67.

Galloway, Alex. 2012. *The Interface Effect*. Cambridge: Polity.

Gross, Matthias. 2010. *Ignorance and Surprise. Science, Society, and Ecological Design*. Cambridge: MIT Press.

Gross, Matthias. 2016. "Risk and ignorance." In *Routledge Handbook of Risk Studies*, edited by Adam Burgess, Alberto Alemanno, and Jens O. Zinn, 310–317. Abingdon: Routledge.

Holl, Ute. 2015. "Media Theory (or, and, despite) a Theory of Cultural Techniques." *Texte zur Kunst* 98: 80–87.

Humphreys, Paul. 2009. "The Philosophical Novelty of Computer Simulation Methods." *Synthese* 169: 615–626.

Laclau, Ernesto. 1996. *Emancipation(s)*. London: Verso.

Lévi-Strauss, Claude. 1987. *Introduction to Marcel Mauss*, edited by Felicity Baker. London: Routledge. (Original French edition: *Introduction a l'oeuvre de Marcel Mauss*. Paris: Presses Universitaires de France, 1950.)

Rouvroy, Antoinette. 2011. "Technology, Virtuality, and Utopia: Governmentality in an Age of Autonomic Computing." In *Law, Human Agency and Autonomic Computing: The Philosophy of Law Meets the Philosophy of Technology*, edited by Antoinette Rouvroy and Mireille Hildebrandt, 119–140. Abingdon: Routledge.

Wehling, Peter. 2009. "Nichtwissen – Bestimmungen, Abgrenzungen, Bewertungen." *Erwägen Wissen Ethik* 20 (1): 95–106.

ARISTOTELES

ROMANTIC COMEDY

IMAGINATION

POETOLOGY OF KNOWLEDGE

ALGORITHMS

POWER

TOM HANKS

[2]

The Total Archive: On the Function of Non-Knowledge in Digital Cultures

Andreas Bernard

This article tries to combine two tendencies in digital cultures. On the one hand, search engines and social media seem to erase former gaps of knowledge that in the history of literature and film, from Sophocles' *Oedipus Rex* to the Hollywood romantic comedy, were crucial to the tragic or comical plots. On the other hand, this abundance of knowledge, all these electronic encyclopedias and social connections in our pockets, is organized by a set of algorithms and computational performances that are unknown and even myterious to their users. The article discusses this simultaneous growth of knowledge and non-knowledge in digital cultures. The total archive of our presence produces new illegibilities.

1

Although the movie is only 15 years old, its story seems to belong to some strange and distant past. *Serendipity*, starring John Cusack and Kate Beckinsale, was one of the most successful box office hits of 2001. In the film, a man and a woman get to know one another by chance while Christmas shopping; after a few intimate hours spent together in Manhattan, the two of them, each in a steady relationship of their own, part ways without even bothering to learn the other's first name. "Do you think," the man asks in parting, "good old fate is just gonna deliver my information right to your doorstep?" The woman then convinces him to write down his full name and telephone number on a five-dollar bill, which she immediately gives away to a street vendor. If they are truly meant for one another, she implies, then the bill containing his information will somehow make it back into her hands. To be fair, she then writes her own name and telephone number inside a book, which, in the same spirit of anonymity and unpredictability, she sells to a used bookstore on the following day. Years go by, and the circulating tokens of love do ultimately bring the destined couple back together, though their reunion occurs shortly before the man's scheduled wedding.

Today, a plot such as *Serendipity*'s would inevitably fall apart not long after the first scene. It is no longer conceivable that two young people would share a nice time together and then part ways without saying "connect with me on Facebook" or having gathered enough information to google each other. Some time ago, the actor Tom Hanks remarked in an interview that the cell phone had ruined many of the traditions of romantic comedy because everyone can call anyone at any time or pictures can be taken that would let the truth out of the bag. In that particular genre, to which Hanks made several of his own successful con-tributions during the 1990s (*Sleepless in Seattle* or *You've Got Mail*), the storylines are typically driven by knowledge gaps: a man and a woman fall in love with one another, but they do so without knowing the other's true identity, or they are separated after a brief encounter. After a series of complications and misunderstandings, they finally come together in a happy ending.

The current media reality has largely eliminated this dramaturgical principle. Stories of this sort are simply no longer thinkable given that smartphones can be consulted at any time. In 1999, it was still more or less possible to transplant Ernst Lubitsch's classic 1940 film *The Shop Around the Corner*, in which two employees who dislike one another unwittingly begin a romantic exchange of letters, into the age of email correspondence. In *You've Got Mail*, Tom Hanks and Meg Ryan can simultaneously fight with each other as business competitors and begin a love affair on the Internet because anonymous chatrooms, misleading AOL addresses, and the lack of search engines still made it possible to conceal one's identity. During the last 15 years, however, throughout which the availability and classification of data have probably brought about greater changes than took place during the 500 years between Gutenberg and Google, it would have been rather silly to revive a plot of this sort: social networks and dating apps have since constrained their users with strict controls over the genuineness and consistency of online profiles. The traditional driving forces behind such movies have thus become ineffective, and in this light it is perhaps no surprise that each of the most successful recent comedies—the *Hangover* trilogy from 2009 to 2013—requires its main characters to have a total blackout after the rowdy night before. Because the Web 2.0 fills in all of the gaps in the characters' knowledge of their everyday activity, drugs and alcohol are all that remains to bring about the amnesia that is so essential to any comedy of errors.

2

To some extent, the following reflections have been inspired by Hanks' remarks. As politicians and economists have repeatedly told us, we are now living in a "knowledge economy." The creation, dissemination, and application of knowledge have long supplanted the production of material goods as the most significant economic factor. Non-knowledge has thus come to be understood more than ever as an unavoidable deficit. The crisis of the "romantic comedy" is only an obvious indication that, wherever possible, a sort of historical countercurrent has also been developing: this countercurrent is characterized by the increasing suspicion among cultural theorists and social scientists that a certain degree of non-knowledge might, in fact, be necessary for the organization and implementation of particular events and processes. In light of our digitally organized culture, I would like to pose the following question: What is the function of non-knowledge as we come closer and closer to producing a total archive of the present?

Since the beginning of this century, steps to fulfill digital technology's ongoing promise of "networking" have been made with remarkable intensity—first, by the establishment of search engines, since 2005, in the form of social media, and most recently by the so-called Internet of Things. Data, people, services, and objects are now constantly connected to one another; according to some of the trendiest terminology, they are said to "communicate," to reveal their location, to "share," and to "be shared." My first interest is thus concerned with the relationship of this ubiquitous networking, which is, of course, also a form of ubiquitous identification, to the history and status of human imagination. On the one hand, this involves an examination of such cultural products as literature and film; on the other hand, however, it also involves an analysis of forms of subjective fantasies, desires, and reminiscences. The latter are not simply arbitrary and timeless emotions; rather, they each have their own pertinent *history*. They react, for instance, to the ways in which technical media happen to transform ideas into realities.

Tracking down the most relevant and effective characters in the
canon of tragedies and comedies makes it immediately clear that
the non-knowledge between the actors has a sort of elementary
significance. Gaps in communication and interrupted connections—either preordained or brought about by intrigue—are
what provide dramas with irreparable guilt or the joy of playfully
resolved misunderstandings.

From Sophocles' *Oedipus Rex* to Shakespeare's tragic and
comic heroes and on through the personae of classical and
late-bourgeois drama, the non-knowledge of the characters
is constitutive for what takes place in the works. Paul Valéry's
dictum that "man can only act because he is capable of not
knowing" is above all an expression of a poetological truth,
and it is telling that the most influential *theoretical* treatments
of the laws of poetry situate this dynamic at the center of their
expositions. "The most powerful elements of emotional interest in tragedy," as Aristotle remarked in his *Poetics*, are "the
reversal of circumstances (*peripeteia*) and the recognition scenes"
(1450a32). According to Aristotle, these turning points in the
story—these "changes from ignorance to knowledge"—constitute
the "foundation" and "soul" of the characters being represented
(1452a).

If it is indeed true that the "romantic comedy" is threatening to
sink forever into the networking maelstrom of digital media, then
this development certainly has much to do with the narrative
stasis caused by exhaustively profiled identities and relationships. On the one hand, it seems as though today's most popular
love stories, such as Pascal Mercier's best-selling *Night Train
to Lisbon*, are only able to maintain their ostensible realism at
the cost of ignoring technological developments (the protagonist's entire journey could just as well have been replaced by a
little Internet research). On the other hand, this stagnation has
resulted in the success of backwards-oriented narrative worlds in
which the current constellations of knowledge do not pertain. The
somewhat disconcerting boom of the fantasy genre in literature,

film, and on television has been going strong for several years—think of the Tolkien renaissance, the spectacular success of the Harry Potter stories, and the universally acclaimed medievalistic television series *Game of Thrones*. I believe it is possible to associate this boom with today's media reality and its narrative and imaginative consequences.

3

As regards non-knowledge, what interests me in a broader sense is an epistemological perspective that could perhaps be called a technological history of imagination—a type of history that is concerned with imagination's architectonic, infrastructural, communications-technical, and transportation-technical conditions at a given time. Such interrelations play not only a significant role in our present day; they were also of great concern, for instance, to the authors writing during the late-eighteenth and early-nineteenth centuries. The latter was an epoch in which many of today's fundamental questions about digital culture were first raised (as Jeannie Moser argues in her contribution to this volume): Should we be enthusiastic or skeptical about encyclopedic projects? What is the relationship between the sovereign subject and overwhelming masses of data? What are the acceptable manners of representing knowledge about human beings?

In a remarkable entry in his "Scrapbooks," written in the 1770s and given the simple title "Novels," Georg Christoph Lichtenberg recorded his reflections about this very issue of the relationship between knowledge, non-knowledge, and the literary imagination. It is worthwhile quoting this passage at some length:

> Our way of life has become so simple now, and all our customs so free of mystery … that a man who wants to write a German novel hardly knows how to bring people together or tie together the knots of a story. Because German mothers today almost always breastfeed their own children,

the possibility of exchanging children has disappeared, and thus a source of literary invention has been obstructed that can hardly be compensated for with any money. ... In England, moreover, chimneys function not merely as channels for smoke but mainly as ventilation shafts in bedrooms, and thus they provide immediate and undetectable access to any given place in a house. ... In Germany, however, a lover would hardly cut a pleasant appearance if he opted to climb down a chimney. ... Finally, a genuine obstacle to intrigue is the otherwise fine and praiseworthy institution of post directors in Germany ... and the fact that, instead of English stagecoaches and machines—in which a pregnant princess would feel neither shame nor fear to travel—we have rather introduced the open-air garbage carts that are so dear to us. The opportunities for mischief provided by these comfortable English coaches do not need to be expressed with words. First of all, if a girl and her lover run away from London in the evening, they could be in France before the father wakes up. ... In Germany, however, even if the father realized that his daughter was missing three days after the fact, it would be enough to know that they traveled with the post in order to catch up with them by horse at the third station. (Lichtenberg 1968, 373–377, translated by the author)

Lichtenberg's concern in this passage is, as he wrote, the "source of literary invention," which can be "obstructed" or expedited by infrastructural realities. The practice of breastfeeding one's own children, which was established in Germany and France during the last quarter of the eighteenth century, the varying sizes of chimneys from one country to another, and the speed of stagecoaches each exert a degree of influence over the narrative possibilities in different national literatures—and, as far as genealogical origins or the escape routes of lovers are concerned, it is always non-knowledge that constitutes the dynamic of a given plot.

26 A few years later, in 1812, Friedrich Schlegel posed a rather similar question in his lectures on the *History of Literature, Ancient and Modern*. In comparison with some of his treasured books such as *Don Quixote*, Schlegel believed that contemporary German fiction was lacking in vitality, and this he attributed to an "all-too-strong and perfected bourgeois order" that had since been established. Inhibited by the "transparency" or "clarity" of present social relations, as Schlegel called them, German novelists were forced to seek "some sort of opening or access into a domain in which fantasy or the imagination can move freely." "The romantic element in many of these second-rate romances," he went on, "seems to coincide very closely with a state of morals disposed to set at defiance magisterial authority." And then he added the following prognosis:

> Whenever the economy of municipal arrangements shall be perfected in general police so as to prevent all contraband trading, and so vigilantly detective as to sketch not only the physiognomy but also the biography of every traveler on his passport, romance will become obsolete, from the want of necessary materials. (Schlegel 1859, 259)[1]

4

As mentioned at the beginning, the productive force of non-knowledge has recently begun to attract a considerable amount of attention in cultural studies and the social sciences. In light of the prominent theoretical impulses of the last few decades, the present interest in non-knowledge seems quite logical; it is a category that has long played an eminent role, at least implicitly. For the fact of the matter is that—in the wake of Canguilhem, Foucault, Kittler, Rheinberger, and rediscovered authors such as Ludwik Fleck—disciplines such as the history of science and

---

1   These passages by Lichtenberg and Schlegel were brought to my attention by Bernd Seiler's fascinating study, *Die leidigen Tatsachen*, published in 1983.

historical epistemology have been characterized by a process
of desemantization: what has taken the place of reconstructing
the scientific truth contents that are overhauled and supplanted
from one author and epoch to the next is, as we all know, a shift
of attention toward the *distribution* of knowledge at a given time,
toward the political or social mechanisms of its verification,
toward the medial and experimental preconditions of cognition
(*Erkenntnis*), and even toward the "poetology" of knowledge,
which—to quote Joseph Vogl's programmatic text—"immediately
connects the production of statements and objects of knowledge
with the question of staging and representability" (1999, 7).

On the one hand, these theoretical premises necessitate that
something else must play an equal role, namely the inverse
of whatever happens to be regarded as true and conducive
to knowledge at a particular time and for particular "styles of
thinking." Any exposure of an "order of discourse" must also take
into account the negative of this order; that is, it has to account
for what has fallen through cracks or has been discarded as
obsolete, faulty, dangerous, or insufficiently validated knowledge.
(To this extent, non-knowledge has always been a component of
every discourse-analytical approach to historiography.) On the
other hand, the most productive research approaches attempt to
convert this epistemological object itself into something positive,
productive, and operational. At issue here is not "ignorance"—
that is, I am not concerned with that which, being in clear
opposition to the known, would thus be false and correctable.
The issue is rather a fundamental gap or *lacuna*, a category
that—beyond the mere negative—casts doubt on the validity
of the oppositions between true and false, representable and
unrepresentable, and thereby generates specific epistemological
effects. "How societies manage their non-knowledge," in the
words of Albrecht Koschorke, "is certainly one of the most difficult
questions of cultural theory" (1999, 445).

It is possible to illustrate this thesis with three short examples: first, of course, with the category of the "secret," which

Georg Simmel long ago praised as the "greatest achievement of mankind" and thus firmly secures the "foundation of the social" in the mode of non-knowledge, both within small groups as well as between nations. The manner in which institutions function—and not only secret societies and intelligence services—is based on intransparency. Among both the proponents and critics of digital culture, however, the secret has a bad reputation. The chief guideline or category is now "transparency," and this is just as apparent in Mark Zuckerberg's pleas for the necessity of global communication as it is in the dissident concept of the "leak," that is, in the unreserved puncturing and exposure of intransparent structures, as demanded by Julian Assange or the European Pirate Parties. These seemingly incongruous ideologies coincide in their absolute trust in the enlightening effects of knowledge and cognition. For both positions, the social significance of the secret is negligible. Regarding where things might lead, however, if the digital world's transparency becomes reality, David Eggers recently offered speculations in his dystopian novel *The Circle*. In his story, the complete openness and transparency of relations dissolve into a totalitarian system, and social terror ensues.

Second, it can be said that even the normative foundations of society are stabilized by non-knowledge. This can be demonstrated by the concept of the "dark or hidden figure of crime," about which the sociologist Heinrich Popitz wrote a magnificent study almost 50 years ago. In order for a state to maintain the "validity of its norms," according to Popitz, it is necessary for it *not* to reveal each of their violations and thus *not* to punish each of their violators. This would be possible from neither an administrative point of view, because the "sanctioning organization" would be overstrained, nor from a moral point of view, because the mass of delinquents would dull society's general readiness to be sanctioned, causing the social norms to lose their "protective function" (Popitz 1968, 16 and 18). From this argument, Popitz derived the idea that a "dark figure" is necessary for a social system to function. It is this hidden figure that, as he wrote, provides "relief from the rigidity and overtaxing nature of the norm by limiting information about behavior." The category of the "dark figure," he concluded, "opens up a sphere in which the system of norms and sanctions does not need to be strictly heeded and yet does not obviously forfeit its claim of validity. ... It enables ... a blurry relation to exist in social life." (Popitz 1968, 12)

Popitz introduced the category of strategic non-knowledge as an antidote to the threat of a "transparent society" (1968, 9). Regarding both Schlegel's remarks and a novel such as *The Circle*, it is telling that Popitz immediately associated the possibility of escaping from the horrific vision of total profiling with the possibility of literary narration. "There will always be," he wrote, "new opportunities to evade the interests of information. Even Orwell could write about his utopia of perfect behavioral information in the form of a novel: the story that he tells can only get underway because the perfection—despite all of the installed surveillance equipment—is not achieved. It is still possible in his story for certain things to be done 'in secret.'" (Popitz 1968, 9)

A third and final example involves a certain *caesura* in our historical knowledge about human beings, a sort of turning point whose questions and consequences warrant further discussion as we find ourselves today on the threshold of digital culture. The turning point in question was the advent of numerical statistics around the year 1800. As Wolfgang Schäffner has noted, it marked a transition from knowledge to "data knowledge" that "formulated epistemological questions no longer on the basis of human capacities such as reason, understanding, or memory but rather on the basis of a specific materiality, ... such as that which appears in the problem of transmitting and storing masses of data" (1999, 124). Long into the nineteenth century, an epistemological ambition persisted that hoped to make the knowledge of a nation seem complete and transparent—in the form of tableaus, for instance. At the beginning of the nineteenth century, however, the excess of data, which, as Schäffner notes, "exceeded the domain of the productive subject" (1999, 123), required a different method—a displacement of descriptive statistics in favor of numerical statistics, which transformed non-knowledge "into an operable space." Instead of a "complete dissemination of all data" there now appeared the "operationalization of the absent" by means of "samples," "large-scale calculations," or "averages" (Schäffner 1999, 123). Thus, to summarize these three brief case studies, non-knowledge became a precondition of the social, a precondition of the narrative, and a precondition of knowledge itself.

5

The organization of knowledge in our present day—based as it is on "Internet protocols," "algorithms," or "Big Data" (and these terms remain puzzling however often they might be cited)—poses these very same questions with a new level of intensity. Where, in our digital culture, can the lines be drawn between knowledge and non-knowledge, between transparency and intransparency, and between predictability and incommensurability? Ubiquitous networking has generated a new and entirely unprecedented excess of available knowledge. Interruption, unfamiliarity, and distance—three of the constitutive conditions of narration—have more or less been eliminated by digital currents of rationalization and data collection. This rationalization also concerns certain fundamental features of our collective imagination—including, for instance, the cultural and social conceptions of love and how to find someone to share it with.

As sociologist Eva Illouz has recently demonstrated with a wealth of evidence, online dating, at least in Western societies, has become the predominate way for single or promiscuous people to find a romantic partner. The agencies behind all of this advertise that they are able to *predict* the likelihood of successful amorous relationships: those who leave enough information about themselves and their wishes in the profiles and multiple-choice questionnaires—or so the promise goes—have the strongest

chance of meeting the right person. "Love is not a coincidence"
reads the seemingly ubiquitous slogan of elitepartner.de. Of
course, this assertion vehemently contradicts the "romantic
code"—to use Luhmannian terms—that has organized the
meeting of couples and the synthesis of love and marriage over
the past 250 years.

The fact that this code is based on contingency and non-
knowledge was made clear by Georg Friedrich Wilhelm Hegel in
a section of his *Aesthetics* entitled, appropriately enough, "Love's
Contingency." Unlike the "objective content of existence, with
one's family, political aims, nation, and professional obligations,"
the romantic feeling is entirely left to the person in love, and
the question of "why it is just this man or this individual woman
alone is grounded in the person's own private character, in the
contingency of caprice" (Hegel 1973, 567). Conversely, Hegel says,
the suffering experienced in pursuit of love, the false selection
of a love interest, or a lack of reciprocation cannot be considered
an "injustice in itself" and a "universal interest." This is because,
he notes, "there is nothing inherently necessary in his taking a
fancy for this girl alone" (Hegel 1973, 568). The idea of romantic
love depends on the unpredictability and irrationality of the
encounter, on the fact that, in the eternal stream of passers-by
and fleeting faces, a particular figure could suddenly appear,
like the "flash of lightning" in Baudelaire's famous poem, and
give new meaning to one's life. In the world of online dating, this
fateful moment is replaced by accurate calculations of data, by
the mathematically supported work of "matching." At the large
dating agencies, potential "hits" and "pairings" are generated less
by the individual profile searches made by clients than they are
by computer programs, which, on the basis of a person's data and
browsing history, are presumably better than the person in question at boiling down his or her own tastes and preferences.

With the rise of online dating, it seems as though the history
of romantic relationships has entered into a new epoch. As is
well known, the era of marriages being determined on social,

religious, and economic grounds lasted until the end of the eighteenth century. The prevailing notion of romance since then—namely the idea that even family-sanctioned partnerships should be based solely on the passionate feelings of two people—seems to be gradually eroding with the collective trust that we are placing in online dating. Search engines and algorithms have become new external authorities for making decisions about the suitability of potential romantic partners. Today it is no longer parents and families that determine which couples should be together; instead, it is the programmers and psychologists employed by dating agencies. In the twenty-first century, the arranged marriage is experiencing an unexpected comeback. No longer occasioned by finances, status, or faith, today's arranged marriages are made only if the data situation is favorable.

6

Digital technology provides us with abundant and omnipresent data that seem to be eliminating all non-knowledge. Every social gathering and every walk in the park now takes place in a fully equipped library, and the emblem of our time seems to be a table at which everyone is turning to a phone or tablet in order to answer or solve, by pushing a few buttons on a screen, whatever questions or problems might have arisen. In conversations, one occasionally still hears the term "walking encyclopedia" applied to people who, when asked, seem to know something about the most esoteric areas of knowledge. Yet this term has now become applicable to every person with a smartphone at his or her disposal; in fact, it doesn't even make sense anymore as a compliment. Moreover, the computer-controlled collection and classification of large amounts of data not only has access to the past and the present; it also, as we hear so often on the news, is used as a method for making allegedly precise predictions about such things as future criminal activity or consumer behavior in particular regions of the country.

Algorithms and Big Data are today's instruments of knowledge—
and yet the ambivalence of digitally construed organizations
of knowledge lies in the fact that, while their *effects*—their
arrangements and distributions—are visible to all of us, the
specific manner in which they function remains opaque. The
ontology of algorithms—of that set of instructions which
determines the series of Google hits, the composition of a
Facebook timeline, or the matches of a dating agency—is a secret
known perhaps to just a few corporate programmers. Or perhaps
it is not even known to them, given that complex and proliferating
computer codes are not exactly represented in a specific way and
that some of them can only be viewed by the initiated at a single
location, much like the well-guarded secret of Coca-Cola's original
recipe.

It would thus seem to be high time for the so-called digital
humanities, which have emerged at our universities over the past
few years, to start reflecting on a *poetology of digital knowledge.*
A perspective of this sort has not received sufficient attention
from those involved in this area of study. The avant-garde's often
blind optimism about knowledge, and the general historical
forgetfulness of projects being undertaken in the humanities
and social sciences—which rely precisely on "data mining" and
computer-generated quantitative processes—are truly quite
striking. In practically all of the articles that have been published in the past years on the use of Big Data, the aim of the
methodology is claimed to be the recognition of "patterns." From
numerous examples, I quote Lev Manovich—certainly one of the
more original thinkers in this regard—who in one of his essays
concludes that the "computer-assisted examination of massive
cultural data sets typically reveals new patterns in this data
which even [the] best manual 'close reading' would miss" (2011,
9). In terms of the history of theory, it seems as though epistemology has regressed by 50 years, back to when Derrida was
writing his notorious article about Lévi-Strauss and reproaching
structuralism for deploying a sort of metaphysics of the concept

of structure which simply shifted that reference, which was presumably at the heart of the entire structuralist enterprise, onto a transcendental signified. Perhaps something similar might apply, for example, to the curves, diagrams, and schemata that are generated when Google's Ngram Viewer is used to chart the frequency of certain words or phrases in tens of thousands of digitalized novels.

As regards the issue of non-knowledge, however, I am more interested in a different aspect of the digital humanities, namely in the breach or discontinuity that exists between the visualizable effects of computer-assisted organizations of knowledge and their codes—the 30-year-old mathematical origins of a programming language that end users have never had to learn, at least not since the first Macintosh computers and their intuitive interface made coding skills unnecessary. The basic question is this: How can algorithms be represented? Thinking about search engines some ten years ago, Peter Haber diagnosed the permanent neglect of any genealogy of knowledge. It is a question that has been addressed more recently by the media philosopher Alexander Galloway: drawing a maybe precarious and assailable distinction, he divides digitally processed knowledge into raw numerical "data" and into "information" that can be represented in writing, images, or videos (it remains doubtful, of course, whether something like "raw data" actually exists). I believe that this distinction is productive, however, because Galloway is able to use it to isolate the rift that exists between mathematically calculated and visualized knowledge. With reference to Gilles Deleuze's famous little essay, he notes: "Adequate visualizations of control society have *not happened*" (Galloway 2011, 91, emphasis original).

It is possible to analyze, for instance, the representation of Edward Snowden's betrayal of secrets, as has been attempted in newspaper reports and in the impressive film *Citizenfour*, precisely in terms of the representivity or non-representivity of digitally mediated masses of data. Glenn Greenwald and Laura

Poitras' encounter with Snowden in a hotel room in Hong Kong
is riveting; having watched the film, you would be able to say
something about the relationship between victimhood and whis-
tleblowing or about the life-changing boldness of Snowden's
act, but you would be at pains to identify any details about the
bold nature of the *content* that Snowden had brought to light.
The film offers no specific image of this excess of abstract and
encoded data. In *Citizenfour*, Poitras repeatedly depicts the
decoded greetings from the beginnings of Snowden's email
correspondence, but then as soon as we expect to see something
decisive, she cuts away from the scene. And so today, when it is
so often said that the collective outrage in the wake of these rev-
elations has been somewhat restrained, the main reason for this
restraint is presumably related to the problem of representation.

To revisit Galloway's thoughts for a final time, the algorithm is
an authority, but its calculus, its governmental principles—its
"algorithmic governmentality," as Antoinette Rouvroy recently
called it—remain in the dark. For most members of the Internet
society, from its indifferent consumers to its political activists,
the world of the digital represents a space of transparency, participation, and freedom—the most modern manifestation of
modernity's achievements. But those examining the relationship
between knowledge and non-knowledge that this space produces
more closely could also come to the conclusion that the 250-year-
old elements of the bourgeois public sphere no longer have much
to do with the way in which digital culture functions. Such is the
remarkable thesis of the article by Claus Pias and Timon Beyes
published in this volume on "Transparency and Secrecy."

If a characteristic of modern organizations of knowledge and
society is that they have replaced both the secretive, arbitrary
rule of the absolute sovereign and providential notions of the
future with concepts of openness, contingency, and participation,
then the premodern world and our digital culture do in fact have
a number of things in common. Algorithms create providence: on
Amazon and Netflix, they tell us which books or television series

might appeal to us after we have made a single purchase; they suggest friends to us on social networks; they select potential marriage partners while the self-empowerment of the romantic and subjective selection of partners, which had been determining the course of love since the last third of the eighteenth century, slowly fades into oblivion.

An analysis of non-knowledge, however, is not at all intended to leave an aftertaste of irrationality. Rather, it should make a contribution to the analysis of power structures in the digital age. As Galloway has written: "The point of unrepresentability is the point of power. And the point of power today is not the image. The point of power today resides in networks, computers, information, and data" (2011, 92).

As authorities over knowledge, the most powerful actors in this sphere are entirely aware of the ancient and grand tradition to which they belong. So much is clear, for instance, in the sovereign playfulness with which they have named themselves. After all, the second *o* in the acronym *Yahoo*, the first mainstream web portal in the history of the Internet, stands for the word *oracle*.

References

Aristotle. 1996. *Poetics*, translated with an introduction and notes by Malcolm Heath. London: Penguin.

Galloway, Alexander. 2011. *The Interface Effect*. Cambridge: Polity Press.

Hegel, Georg Wilhelm Friedrich. 1973. *Aesthetics: Lectures on Fine Art*, Volume 1. Oxford: Oxford University Press.

Koschorke, Albrecht. 1999. *Körperströme und Schriftverkehr: Mediologie des 18. Jahrhunderts*. München: Wilhelm Fink Verlag.

Lichtenberg, Georg Christoph. 1968. "Romane." In idem. *Schriften und Briefe*, Volume 1, edited by Wolfgang Promies, 373–377. München: Carl Hanser Verlag.

Manovich, Lev. 2011. "Trending: The Promises and Challenges of Big Social Data." Accessed February 20, 2017. http://manovich.net/content/04-projects/067-trending-the-promises-and-the-challenges-of-big-social-data/64-article-2011.pdf.

Popitz, Heinrich. 1968. *Über die Präventivwirkung des Nichtwissens: Dunkelziffer, Norm und Strafe*. Tübingen: Mohr Siebeck Verlag.

Schäffner, Wolfgang. 1999. "Nicht-Wissen um 1800." In *Poetologien des Wissens um 1800*, edited by Joseph Vogl, 123–144. München: Wilhelm Fink Verlag.

Schlegel, Friedrich. 1859. *Lectures on the History of Literature, Ancient and Modern*.
London: G. Bell & Sons Pages.

Vogl, Joseph. 1999. "Einführung." In *Poetologien des Wissens um 1800*, edited by
Joseph Vogel, 7–18. München: Wilhelm Fink Verlag.

SECRECY

ARCANE

TRANSPARENCY

PARTICIPATION

TEMPORALITY

TIME

DIGITAL CULTURES

[3]

Secrecy, Transparency, and Non-Knowledge

Timon Beyes and Claus Pias*

WikiLeaks, the Snowden affair, and secret service hacks have brought the notion of the secret, long sidelined by a morally charged discourse on digital transparency, to the forefront of the world's attention. Correspondingly, in this chapter we conceptualize digital cultures not—or at least not primarily—in terms of the nature and potential of transparency (or of related concepts such as participation and the public sphere). Instead, we suggest thinking about them in terms of the secret, in terms of fundamental intransparency and non-knowledge, and in terms of the arcane. How would digital cultures be understood if we set aside modern concepts and instead examine them through the strangeness of premodern concepts like the arcane?

If it is true that transparency represents one of today's most prominent concepts, then digitalization can be said to designate the media-technological condition of its ubiquity. As Manfred Schneider has pointed out, during the last 20 years or so a "messianic potential" has consolidated in the ideal and ideology of transparency (Schneider 2013, 13). This corresponds approximately to the span of time in which forms of digital world-making have prevailed, forms whose technological basis has come to characterize the systems and processes of communication, perception, and the bestowal of meaning (*Sinngebung*) (Striphas 2015). This development has made it clear that we have to speak of digital cultures in the plural, if only because the heterogeneity of this socio-technical arrangement seems to correspond to various forms of world-making that have arisen in tandem with the digital media environment that now pervades our lifeworld.

In opposition to the messianism of transparent and secret-free spheres of, say, politics and business, which derives its energy from the Internet's fiber-optic cables and the omnipresence of intelligent artifacts that can, in part, communicate with one another without the intervention of human subjects, there stands the nightmare of a "transparency society," in which the exposed lives of individuals become "big data" in the hands of Internet companies and government intelligence agencies that, while remaining intransparent themselves, collect and evaluate the traces left behind by digital users (Han 2015; Pasquale 2015). Activists, in turn, have been experimenting with media-technically enabled tactics of intransparency and secrecy in order to make it possible for user-based representations of identity to escape into anonymity or into subject positions that are fluctuating and temporary (the group known as "Anonymous" has thus far been the most captivating example of this; see Coleman 2015). The whole affair with Edward Snowden and the

---

*   Parts of this chapter are taken in revised form from the forthcoming "The Media Arcane." A prior version of the text was first published in German in *Zeitschrift für Kulturwissenschaften* 2014 (2): 111–117.

US National Security Agency (NSA), moreover, has certainly con- firmed Schneider's laconic dictum: "In the here and now, there is no transparency" (Schneider 2013, 14).

At the same time, Snowden's betrayal of secrets has brought the very concept of the secret, so long sidelined by the morally charged discourse in favor of digital transparency, to the fore- front of our attention. Our contribution to this debate is devoted to conceptualizing digital cultures not—or at least not primarily— in terms of the problematic nature and potential of transparency (or of related concepts such as participation and the public sphere) but rather to thinking about them in terms of the secret, in terms of fundamental intransparency, and in terms of the arcane.[1] Our first step will thus be to (re)call to mind the general social form—at least beyond its commonly understood ethical dubiousness—of the secret and its functionality; this will allow us to shed a more sobering light on secrecy and its betrayal. We would then like to venture an experimental-historical approach in greater detail, which will enable us to reexamine, with reference to premodern types of secrets, the present state of digital cultures on the basis of their temporal structures. There are thus two sides to our suggested approach: On the one hand, it is con- cerned with the question of how digital cultures can be concep- tualized in terms of the secret; on the other hand, however, it is also concerned with whether our present concepts of the secret are even appropriate for or conducive to this type of thinking.

For reflecting on the social form of the secret, Georg Simmel's meandering essay on "the secret and secret society" marks an invaluable point of departure. Independent of their contents or the value attributed to them, Simmel considered "the attractions

---

1   Based on a similar argument, Howard Caygill recently suggested turning
     to the notions of secrecy and the arcane for rethinking the relation-
     ship between state and civil society: "Any radical politics founded in the
     emergent global civil society empowered by but also dependent on digital
     technology has to confront the problem of the *arcana* of state and civil
     society …" (2015, 38; original emphasis).

of secrecy" to be a necessary aspect for differentiating social relations; secrecy's attractions are enabled by differentiation as much as they intensify them (1999, 409). The secret, "or the concealment of realities through negative or positive means, is one of mankind's greatest achievements. Unlike the childish condition in which every idea is given immediate expression and every activity is put on display for everyone, the secret leads to an immense enhancement of life, and this is because so many of life's contents cannot even emerge in circumstances of complete publicity" (Simmel 1999, 406). To write the history of secrecy is thus one way of tracing the development of society: a sequence of revealed things that have become secret and of secret things that have been revealed. This yields a sort of zero-sum game of incoming and outgoing contents that are worthy of confidentiality, of secrecy and revelation, covertness and betrayal, with the secret functioning as the mysterious operator of social evolution.

In light of today's digital cultures, however, it is reasonable to call into question Simmel's concluding speculation that the "activities of the general public will become ever more open as those of individuals become more secretive" (1999, 411). Is the self-exposure of digital users on the Internet not indicative of the porous nature of the distinction between the public and the private, and does the discovery of secret masses of data by WikiLeaks and Snowden—their publication aside—not prove the existence of an enormous apparatus of secrecy? That said, Simmel's basic idea still seems rather fruitful to us, namely that the secret deserves to be taken seriously as a fundamental category of cultural analysis. What is needed is a historical investigation of various forms of secrecy in order to gain insight into its present-day varieties (Assmann and Assmann 1997–1999). From a historical perspective, moreover, it will be shown that the secret ought to be thought about somewhat differently: The question is not what is being kept secret but what *is able* to be betrayed and what—in light of this ability or inability to be an object of

betrayal—constitutes the significance and the logic of the secret
in various cultures and at various times (Horn 2013).

In this sense, we would like to propose a thought experiment, and it is to think about digital cultures beyond any concept of modernity according to which digital cultures are themselves modernity's final product, and have possibly even brought an end to the very modernity in question (Lyotard 1984). Many of today's passionate debates, it seems, have illustrated this issue by means of a latent anachronism that finds expression through the use of established concepts such as transparency, the public sphere, and participation (Baxmann et al. 2016). To intensify and take this anachronism further: How would digital cultures be understood if we set aside modern concepts (and ever-derivative postmodern concepts) and instead examined them through the strangeness of premodern concepts? For at that time the secret possessed an altogether different and, at least for our purposes, potentially fruitful historical semantics.

Up until the seventeenth century, cosmology drew a line around an essentially secretive realm, a line that demarcated a fundamental unknown in the form of natural secrets. It was modern science that first raised an objection to such secrets, namely with the goal of gaining knowledge about nature with natural means and of removing all authority from the "cosmic-religious stop sign" (Luhmann and Fuchs 1989, 104). Using the language of systems theory, we might say that time yielded the possibility of de-paradoxing natural secrets. In a comparable manner, however, "high" matters of state were regarded, on the basis of their nature, as secretive. Here the resolutions, decisions, and deeds enacted by the lords of wisdom were thought to possess a secret and essentially unfathomable intelligence, without which the stability of the state could not be preserved. The resolutions, decisions, and deeds themselves were clear for all to see, but the reasons behind them *could* not be betrayed and thus could also not be discussed. In cosmological terms, they were as incommunicable as all the great matters of nature and therefore they represented not only wisdom, the arbitrary nature of which "has to be protected from triviality and thus kept secret" (Luhmann and Fuchs 1989, 116), but also a structurally *unbetrayable* secret.

In this context, the treatment of the secret then was probably more differentiated than it is today (or in Simmel's sketch of things), and this is because premodernity was familiar with various types of secrets—such as the *arcana cordis*, the *arcana dei*, the *arcana mundi*, or the *arcana imperii*—each of which obeyed different concepts, methods, and rationalities. As far as our argument is concerned, however, the primary distinction to keep in mind is that between the *mysterium* (something non-knowable and thus non-betrayable) and the *secretum* (something concealed that can be made intelligible and thus be betrayed). The *arcana imperii* thus incorporate both aspects: the *mysterium* of the ruler's wisdom and caprice as the center of an unbetrayable reasoning and, at the same time, a bustling multiplicity of minor or major *secreta* that are the object of betrayal and of efforts to keep them secret from all sorts of "intelligence" (literally, that is, from essentially possible forms of insight).

In contrast to this, the debates held today among politicians and in the newspapers concerning data protection and privacy rights operate with a different—and from our perspective rather reductive—variety of secrets, namely with those that can be betrayed. As soon as the shift is made into this modern category, a secret can either be betrayed or not betrayed, revealed or kept confidential. Without this hegemony of a particular type of secret, the idea of transparency associated with the so-called bourgeois public sphere could never have been formulated. It is the type of secret that can and must be revealed, and it simultaneously creates a situation in which it is unclear whether the state should fear its citizens or vice versa. With this newfound suspicion of sovereignty, along with an active interest in de-masking arcana, the type of secret that is unbetrayable seems either to have been lost or relocated to another realm.

As Reinhart Koselleck has shown, the unbetrayable secret has
been sublimated into a new temporal order (2004). To some
extent, modernity has transferred the unbetrayable secret of
sovereignty onto time itself. It is the future that has henceforth
become a secret that cannot be betrayed. Moreover, modernity
has firmly associated the question of the future with the notion
of participation and the public sphere. Both are embedded in a
context of secrecy and transparency that are oriented toward the
future. Otherwise participation—according to our modern understanding of it—would be meaningless, because it takes place
between what *is* and what *ought to be*: between how the world
is and how it (otherwise) *could be*. In this sense, as is well known,
the eighteenth century invented a new form of historicity and
thus a new form of history itself. And it came to treat the present
as the decisive place between the "space of experience" and the
"horizon of expectation" (Koselleck 2004, 255–275), as the venue
of an essentially *open* future.

As regards digital cultures, the thesis that we would like to
advance is that a new temporal order has been established—a
"chronotope" that is distinct from the temporal order that
established itself between 1780 and 1830 and has since defined
our thinking. We believe that the beginnings of this change can
be traced back to the rise of modern cybernetics after 1945.
As Norbert Wiener suspected as early as 1948, the advent of
digital computers—along with concepts such as feedback, self-
regulating systems, and prediction—initiated a fundamental
rearrangement of temporal structures (1961, 60–94). With the
digitalization of further aspects of our lifeworld and with the
countless number of apparatuses that can communicate with
one another independently and can—the largest and smallest
alike—control one another mutually and provide feedback to
one another, these particularly cybernetic temporal relations
have more or less become absolute. Arguably, they engender
an order of time in which modern historicity collapses. One
could perhaps call this an "absolutism of the present" (to adapt a

phrase by Robert Musil), or, in Hans Ulrich Gumbrecht's terms, it could be referred to as a "broad present" (2014). The cybernetic chronotope of digital cultures thus raises, yet again, as a topic of discussion the question of historical temporalities.

This diagnosis is not new. A quarter of a century ago, for instance, Vilém Flusser offered a similar interpretation (1991). If, according to Flusser, a bond exists between cybernetic machines that interconnect by means of feedback, that behave adaptively, that process interferences independently, and that allow, by means of what today is called big data, the data traces of subjects to be conflated with the prediction of forms of subjectivation—then the relation between what is and what ought to be collapses and thus, with it, the modern concept of the future. Like other thinkers before and after him, Flusser referred to this condition as "post-history." For logical reasons, according to his diagnosis, there can no longer be any conventionally understood arguments, critiques, or politics within this new temporal order. And thus participation, as Flusser quite radically infers, is "nonsense."[2] In contrast to this bleak outlook, we would like to propose an experimental-historical approach, and this is to think about today's digital cultures precisely *not* in terms of modern concepts but rather—at least tentatively—in terms of premodern concepts. For if the modern temporal order has in fact become problematic or has even collapsed entirely, the challenge would then consist of no longer conceptualizing digital cultures with the categories of transparency, participation, and the public sphere but rather in terms of a fundamental intransparency—in terms, that is, of the arcane.

If the origin of this new temporal order can be ascribed to the cybernetic concepts of feedback, self-regulating systems,

2   In what follows, Flusser then elaborates that figures such as functionaries, depressed people, terrorists, technocrats, and environmental activists are social types that are specific to a present in which participation has become logically impossible.

prediction, and digital computers, then we can state at the same time that digital and networked media are the agents of this chronotope. The everyday examples are countless: Entire industries have since arisen that are concerned with predicting such things as what type of music we like to listen to, which television series we like to watch, who we should really be friends with, or how we can best avoid traffic on our way to work. With greater and greater masses of data, it is becoming increasingly probable to predict even the seemingly unpredictable twists and turns of the subject—something like anticipating the evasive, zig-zag maneuvers of an enemy airplane. It is no longer possible to escape from ourselves; rather, we are incessantly confronted with ourselves and with our own surprising predictability. Being deprived of the future in such ways—this blending of the "space of experience" and the "horizon of expectation" into a media-technical feedback loop between the past and the future—can perhaps better be understood with premodern concepts of time.

Consequently, the thesis can also be advanced that the "like" culture of so-called social media has less to do with modern participation than it does with premodern rituals. "Likes" seem to resemble instead the états, *cortes*, or parliaments that were common from the late Middle Ages until the eighteenth century. Such forms of "participation," to which modernity had put an end, were rituals of *consensus* and not negotiations of *dissent*. It was just such rituals, in fact, that modernity disavowed as the opposite of the political. They operated according to a sort of logic that has nothing to do with a participatory public sphere based on arguments and transparency. They were necessary and performative forms of participation within a non-future-oriented temporal order because they lacked the concept of decision-making itself (Krischer 2010).

These examples, to which many more could be added, raise the question of how much one can and must know about the "apparatuses" (in Flusser's terms) that create the particular temporality of digital cultures, the question of which secrets they

48   might possess that perhaps ought to be made transparent, and the paradoxical question of which secrets they are hiding that are unbetrayable or should perhaps remain protected. To this extent, our attempt at interpretation will either stand or fall depending on the issue of the "understanding" of digital media. And this "media-understanding," as Friedrich Kittler surmised some 30 years ago, is perhaps a melancholy enterprise. His famous pronouncement that media "determine our situation" was made at a moment in which, in light of the emergence of digital cultures, the limitations or the impossibility of our ability to understand them were already beginning to loom. Or in Kittler's own words: "The general digitization … erases the differences among individual media. … [A] total media link on a digital base will erase the very concept of medium. Instead of wiring people and technologies, absolute knowledge will run as an endless loop" (Kittler 1999, 1–2).

Since then, the plea for new types of representation, and even for a new poetics of rendering intelligible network-based governance and control (Galloway 2011), can thus be understood as an effort to oppose the intransparency, unrepresentability, and incommensurability of algorithms with a different "understanding" of digital media and to respond to the absolutism of the present with new images and forms of thinking that go beyond the mere betrayal of *secreta* (à la Snowden) and do greater justice to the *mysterium* of a media-technically conditioned *arcanum*. Especially at stake here is the related issue of action, and the basis for action if this is to take place in a chronotope that, to re-quote Flusser, is no longer determined by transparency, capable of deliberative reasoning, or open to the future. The discourse about transparency, which is always making or reflecting an ethical claim, has reached the limits of a secret that is challenging us to conceptualize an ethics without transparency and a future without the modern understanding of participation and the public sphere (Latour 2003; Foerster 2003).

A look at climatology is especially striking in this context, for
hardly any other domain of knowledge is epistemologically so
dependent on the historical state of hardware and software,
on the observable leaps in quality enabled by sheer computing
power but also on a history of software in whose millions of
lines of poorly documented or undocumented code have sed-
imented archaeological layers of scientific thinking that, for good
reason, cannot be touched or rewritten but merely expanded
and globally standardized and certified. That which is processed
in the supercomputers of such a global research alliance can
simply no longer be made transparent—not even to the scientists
involved. It follows that the habitual routines of critique are at
a loss to address the kind of alternative worlds (and not merely
prognoses) that result, and what might guide our behavior and
self-perception under these conditions. The common reflex of
citing the "constructedness" of knowledge achieves little in this
regard, for it does not absolve anyone from acting in the face of
scenarios that are conscious of their own constructivism. And the
falsifiability of classical scientific ethics (not merely for reasons of
capacity but for systematic reasons as well) is not practicable in
this case because it is impossible to experiment with the climate
as an object of science.

Accordingly, some climate scientists have begun to call for a new
cosmology in order to justify our future activity on a global level.
Should this demand be extended to all possible fields in which
the degree of networking, computer power, and software development has achieved a measure of complexity at which understanding and comprehension are impossible—to such fields that,
nevertheless, create a feedback loop between the present and
the future? If, as in this example, the political becomes entwined
around a center of non-knowledge and non-understanding, a
modern transparency concept of knowledge reaches its limits, as
does the idea of participation by means of voicing one's opinion
about "the matter at hand" (Schelsky 1965). And even this can
be expressed, with recourse to thinking about the secret, in

premodern terms: The legitimation strategy of the computer-simulated climate cosmology corresponds to the premodern political register of sovereignty. Climate research, as it were, has become a new *science royale*. In the place once occupied by the wisdom (or caprice) of the ruler—a place protected by a metaphysical limit to knowledge—there is now the sovereignty of data processing. The sovereignty of data processing has drawn a new line to demarcate that which is constitutively evasive on account of being secretive according to its "nature." Only it is no longer nature and no longer cosmology, but rather technology. Previously, and with respect to sovereign rule, this was referred to as the arcane.

References

Assmann, Aleida, and Jan Assmann. 1997–1999. *Schleier und Schwelle*. 3 vols. München: Wilhelm Fink Verlag.

Baxmann, Inge, Timon Beyes, and Claus Pias, eds. 2016. *Social Media – New Masses*. Zürich: diaphanes (with University of Chicago Press).

Caygill, Howard. 2015. "Arcanum: The Secret Life of State and Civil Society." In *The Public Sphere from Outside the West*, edited by Divya Dwivedi and Sanil V, 21–40. London: Bloomsbury.

Coleman, Gabriella. 2015. *Hacker, Hoaxer, Whistleblower, Spy: The Many Faces of Anonymous*. London: Verso.

Flusser, Vilém. 1991. *Gesten: Versuch einer Phänomenologie*. Düsseldorf: Bollmann.

Foerster, Heinz von. 2003. *Understanding Understanding: Essays on Cybernetics and Cognition*. New York: Springer.

Galloway, Alexander. 2011. "Are Some Things Unrepresentable?" *Theory, Culture & Society* 28: 85–102.

Gumbrecht, Hans Ulrich. 2014. *Our Broad Present: Time and Contemporary Culture*. New York: Columbia University Press.

Han, Byung-Chul. 2015. *The Transparency Society*, translated by Erik Butler. Stanford: Stanford University Press.

Horn, Eva. 2013. *The Secret War: Treason, Espionage, and Modern Fiction*, translated by Geoffrey Winthrop-Young. Evanston: Northwestern University Press.

Kittler, Friedrich. 1999. *Gramophone, Film, Typewriter*, translated by Geoffrey Winthrop-Young and Michael Wutz. Stanford: Stanford University Press.

Koselleck, Reinhard. 2004. *Futures Past: On the Semantics of Historical Time*, translated by Keith Tribe. New York: Columbia University Press.

Krischer, André. 2010. "Das Problem des Entscheidens in systematischer und historischer Perspektive." In *Herstellung und Darstellung von Entscheidungen:*

Verfahren, Verwalten und Verhandeln in der Vormoderne, edited by André Krischer and Barbara Stollberg-Rilinger, 35–64. Berlin: Duncker und Humblot.

Latour, Bruno. 2003. "Why Has Critique Run Out of Steam? From Matters of Fact to Matters of Concern." *Critical Inquiry* 30: 225–248.

Luhmann, Niklas, and Peter Fuchs. 1989. *Reden und Schweigen*. Frankfurt am Main: Suhrkamp.

Lyotard, Jean François. 1984. *The Postmodern Condition: A Report on Knowledge*, translated by Geoff Bennington and Brian Massumi. Manchester: Manchester University Press.

Pasquale, Frank. 2015. *The Black Box Society: The Secret Algorithms that Control Money and Information*. Cambridge, MA: Harvard University Press.

Schelsky, Helmut. 1965. "Der Mensch in der wissenschaftlichen Zivilisation." In idem. *Auf der Suche nach Wirklichkeit: Gesammelte Aufsätze*, 439–480. Düsseldorf: Eugen Diederichs.

Schneider, Manfred. 2013. *Transparenztraum: Literatur, Politik, Medien und das Unmögliche*. Berlin: Matthes & Seitz.

Simmel, Georg. 1999. *Soziologie: Untersuchungen über die Formen der Vergesell-schaftung* (first edition 1908). 3rd ed. Frankfurt am Main: Suhrkamp.

Striphas, Ted. 2015. "Algorithmic Culture." *European Journal of Cultural Studies* 18: 395–412.

Wiener, Norbert. 1961. *Cybernetics: Or Control and Communication in the Animal and the Machine*. 2nd ed. Cambridge, MA: MIT Press.

NON-KNOWLEDGE

PRACTICE OF CRITIQUE

DIGITAL CULTURES

PERFORMING

DISPOSITIF OF TECHNOSPHERES

EXAGGERATED AFFIRMATION

TECHNO-ECOLOGY

[4]

Trickster, Owlglass Pranks, and Dysfunctional Things: Non-Knowledge and Critique in Digital Cultures

Martina Leeker

Non-knowledge and incomprehensibility are, for now, the norm in digital cultures. These states, produced part technologically, part discursively, need particular attention because they form a "politics of non-knowledge." Against this backdrop, critique is necessary but is at the same time difficult to execute because the possibility of gaining knowledge is fundamentally put into question. A performing "practice of critique," which tests the contemporary theorization on digital cultures by reflecting it with exaggerated affirmation and identification, is recommended as a method of critique in digital cultures. Its aim is to enable a self-awareness of digital cultures concerning the politics of non-knowledge.

Introduction

Digital cultures are characterized, it could be argued, by a variety of forms and levels of non-knowledge[1] and incomprehensibility.[2,3] They arise from the technological conditions of digital cultures, about which no one is fully informed, as e.g., unrepresentable algorithms (Galloway 2011) or untestable simulations (Vehlken 2016). Against this background, Timon Beyes and Claus Pias (2014) have proclaimed a culture of non-knowledge and incomprehensibility in digital cultures. That is, they are the norm and demand different forms of participation and policy than e.g., transparency, which is claimed in the dispute over data surveillance. In digital cultures, incomprehensibility and non-knowledge are, it could be said, no longer a shortcoming or an exceptional situation that must be rectified. Rather, they are becoming the status quo, and as such are extremely productive

1   Knowledge refers to Michael Foucault's order of knowledge (episteme) in a historical phase and is inseparable from power (Foucault 1994). Non-knowledge is thereby productive in the sense that through interplay with power, new forms of knowledge can be initiated. An example would be disciplinary actions with which new knowledge for classifying and treating individuals can be created (Foucault 1994). In digital cultures, non-knowledge becomes a new episteme, thus building new knowledge forms.

2   It is possible to know something without understanding it. Understanding then refers first to an operationalization of knowledge regulated by communication and action. Secondly, of interest here, "understanding" refers to the tradition of hermeneutics, organizing the capabilities of cognition and giving sense. This brings to the fore either subjects and deep psychological explanation models, or a machinic understanding that processes data beyond subjects and intentions. Niklas Luhmann's (2001) hermeneutic model, too, requires no subject as it creates understanding as a function of systems over couplings. For Derrida, understanding and hermeneutics are ultimately a problem because they fix definitions and thereby exclude "other" (Derrida and Gadamer 2004). (For the history of hermeneutics in consideration of digital cultures, see Pias 2015.)

3   Knowledge and understanding, or their impossibility, can be brought together under the concept of "knowledge systems," which includes epistemes, epistemology and hermeneutics.

since they produce governmentality, generate subjects, and correspond to the epistemological constitution of digital cultures.

This culture of non-knowledge and incomprehensibility
requires new forms of critique. Critique, tasked with analysis
and reflection, is central to the scientific examination of digital
cultures. Hitherto, to do so was enabled by a presupposed critical
distance, an external position, and an exposure of knowledge
that lay hidden in the background. But where on the one hand
comprehension is supposed to be absent, and when, on the other
hand, human actors are assumed to be already always entangled *in* the technological environment (Engemann and Sprenger
2015b), forms and methods of reflection and critique other
than the traditional ones based on distance to the socio-cul-
tural surroundings must be devised and tested. A contradictory
situation emerges in which notions and practices of critique are
changed under technological conditions and, at the same time,
have the status of discursive assumptions.[4] The aim of this text
is not to find the correct notion of critique but to understand the
discursively generated state of the art of critique under the conditions of digital cultures and how to deal with it.

As a method of dealing with this situation a "practice of critique"
is proposed and explored here with a practical project. In it,
technological conditions and discourses on digital cultures
are embodied and performed. This gives rise to critique and
reflection produced in an "outside in inside" as a proposal for
a model of critique in digital cultures. That this practice could
be successful is due to a specific situation in digital cultures—a
situation constituted of an inescapable ambivalence in which
affirmative new descriptions of digital cultures, technological

4   In this text it is presumed that critique does not exist a priori. On the con-
     trary, there are different concepts and practices of critique in different
     techno-historical situations, which should enable reflection and dis-
     tanciation. This involves the idea that critique is possible from an outer,
     distant position as well as e.g., the concept of a second-order observation,
     which denies any outer position of critique.

procedures, and a politics and economy of affect (Angerer 2007) and relations as a discourse of the new solely valid mode of existence (see Barad 2003) co-exist. Out of this co-existence a "dispositif of technospheres" arises that targets, above all, the ensnarement of human actors in technological environments; a process for which non-knowledge and incomprehensibility are the lifeblood, so to speak. There are, nevertheless, gaps, ruptures, and contradictions in the coexistence in which the practice of critique can take root. Against this background, the performative tests of theories, discourses, and technological conditions for digital cultures should enable the exploration of governmental and subject-forming consequences of the dispositif of the technospheres, which serve at the same time as the basis for other theoretical formations than those of, e.g., non-knowledge and incomprehensibility. Finally, methods of "in/forming culture" are proposed to open temporary gaps for knowledge and for the power to act for human agents.[5]

What's going on? Discourse-on-Things, Techno-Ecology, Digital Mysterium, Dispositif of Technospheres

The current situation of digital discourses on digital cultures can be described as a complex farrago. The interplay of technological procedures and conditions with the discursive generation of digital cultures and economic and political interests form what is called here a "dispositif of technospheres." This dispositif and its constitution in, as well as its benefits from, non-knowledge and incomprehensibility, are outlined below. A crux is the crucial element: non-knowledge and incomprehensibility are

---

5   As the notion "actor" still implies the concept of an autonomous and intentional subject, which is put into question in digital cultures and their "agencies" of different parts, the notion of "human agents" is used to indicate a new status of the older anthropocentric view.

symptoms of digital cultures, yet also discursive inventions that
are of use in the facilitation of governmental forms and economic regimes in digital cultures. These conditions generate a
permanent balancing act in the scientific examination that flips
between critical analysis and discursive generation. To deal with
this situation, the current discourse landscape of cultural and
media studies is presented and analyzed.[6] This is based on non-
knowledge and incomprehensibility, which are quietly escalating
to a "regime of non-knowledge."

Discourse-on-Things and Techno-Ecology

A powerful discourse field within the emerging "regime of non-
knowledge" is formed from discourse-on-things (Latour and
Weibel 2005) and techno-ecology (Hörl 2011), as presented by,
for example, Mark B. Hansen (2011), Erich Hörl (2014) and the
so-called new materialism (Barad 2003). The departure point is
a model according to which human agents and technical things
should no longer be in an instrumental relationship, but instead
bound in a symmetrical agency. Then, as the technologically
based insight suggests, the so-called smart things look back at
human beings and respond to them in a manner that is proactive
and predictive. Paradigmatic in this discourse from the techno-
ecological perspective are the media-neuro-philosophical
assumptions of Mark B. Hansen (2011). He is concerned with an
"environmental media theory," in which humans are an integral
part of a large, networked structure of technological forces and
effects that exists and operates beyond human perception. To
this belong smart technologies such as e.g., sensors that are
themselves a sub-organismal sentience. Description and analysis
of these impels, according to Hansen, humans and subjects
to be regarded not as autonomous entities, but as parts of an
enormous cosmic network of pure potentiality of sensations and

---

6   In further research the technological conditions of digital cultures should be
     delineated from their technical history (*Technikgeschichte*).

events. Technological environments are seen as a power of acting via affecting that can no longer cognitively be grasped or controlled by humans.

What is now crucial is that these discourses affirm the states of impaired comprehension and precarious knowledge, and dignify them. Addressing relationships, understood as operators for an existential involvement of human agents in technological environments, the theories outlined can be seen as a solution for dealing with current challenges. This includes, for example, the (climate) catastrophes and capitalist crises (Hörl 2014; Latour 2010 and 2013), proclaimed with the Anthropocene. Considering that the discourses on relations correspond to the liquidation of an anthropology of autonomous and self-conscious beings, these discourses may well be seen as attempts to solve these crises by installing an environmental modesty. In addition, in the discourse-on-things and in the techno-ecology, a life with the non-comprehensible as the norm is recognized and celebrated, as stated by Bruno Latour: "Once again, our age has become the age of wonder at the *disorders* of nature" (Latour 2010, 481). The being in agencies, because the co-existence of non-human and human actants is no longer predictable or controllable, should moreover correspond to a deliverance from, according to Latour (2008), a "false" history of the human-thing relationship that had been in force since the eighteenth century. It was based on the fact that people saw themselves as independent of their environment and capable of knowledge. Finally, the dissolving of knowledge in sensing and pre-consciousness, thus in non-knowledge as a mode of existence, is ennobled. This process is put forward with, to be specific, an undertone of affirmation (Hansen 2011), as if a more appropriate picture of human agents would now be produced. Non-knowledge and incomprehensibility are produced as conditions for the possibility of "better and more accurate" descriptions of "human" and "existence," as well as the savior of humanity and the earth. This supercharging is what makes it so difficult to build a critical distance from the techno-ecological field of discourse.

Digital Mysterium

From the tradition of media-historically and media-epistemologically oriented media studies comes another proposal for the new description, which is presented in the example of a short essay by Beyes and Pias (2014).[7] It deals with an arcana of digital cultures constituted of secrets that cannot be revealed (un-betrayable secrets).

Pias has proposed the development of a theory of digital cultures whose constitution draws from incomprehensibility and secrets (2016). The big challenge of digital cultures is, specifically, their immanence, since there would no longer be any outside and we would be in technology. This constitution would be attended by an epistemological rupture. In place of hermeneutics would be constitutive incomprehensibility, which could no longer be ignored or escaped (Pias 2015). So it is that, for example, due to the unfathomable amounts of data being processed, no understanding is possible. The programs that process these data are no longer completely comprehensible in their functions and regularities to programmers or scientists. Networks for data transfers in infrastructures (Engemann and Sprenger 2015a) cannot be controlled and could never be if they are going to function at all. Finally, technical things can work in a self-organized way without any human intervention. With this comes to an end a critical hermeneutics in media studies, which while not believing in an understanding in the sense of intrapsychic systems and processes in individuals, probably did believe in the possibility of seeing media effects and works (McLuhan 1964; Kittler 1986). The prerequisite for this "insight" were the codes or the moments of technological upheaval being looked at (Pias

---

7   See the essay by Beyes and Pias in this volume.

2015). This retrospective interpretability is profoundly questioned (Beyes and Pias 2014).

Therefore, Beyes and Pias (2014) argue for a theory of the mystery of digital cultures. Unlike betrayable secrets (*secreta*) the mystery denotes its own constitutional ineluctability. Because it has its history in the concept of a sovereign ruler or cosmology of pre-modern times, which were not meant to be understood, the reasons for the conditions or the decisions are not laid bare and also could not be made transparent.

As an example of a mystery in digital cultures, Beyes and Pias cite climate research (2014), in which the calculations cannot be understood but are, nevertheless, determined to be non-experimentally testable predictions of reality. Instead of a mystery in the form of a ruler or a cosmology of pre-modern times, there is now the secret of data processing.

Interplay: In the Dispositif of Technospheres

The thesis is that the two discursive formations can be bundled into a "dispositif of technospheres." In it, non-knowing and incomprehensibility are affirmed and made productive, or exploited in their productivity. Where the theory of techno-ecology brings in agencies and technological environments, and a new, weak sense of deep-sensory techno-participation (Hörl 2014 and 2016), the cultures of secrets deal with the end of participation and come up with the subordination of human agents under technological regimes. At first glance, the discursive formations therefore exclude themselves. A closer inspection, though, reveals that both are in agreement on a deprivation of "human" power and an inauguration of potent technology. The generator of this change is, in both cases, the secret. Techno-ecology deals with the secret that comes out of the not recognizing and non-knowing of technological spheres. The theory of the digital mysterium has to do with the secret of power and the fascination of non-knowing.

It is about the sphere of non-visible processes and events, which could only be divined.

These new, so-called weak ontologies could be seen as a response to the self-induced crises of digital cultures resulting from technological conditions and their theoretical descriptions. They bring with them to the technospheres the promise of giving humans a position, and a form of action-possibility beyond knowledge, thinking, and awareness, which come out of the extensive "sensing" and the mysterious fanning of the hidden power of technology as the new sovereign. In the techno-ecological, almost animistic, resonance, human agents could operate directly in this dispositif, even when no longer controllable. In contrast to this participative sensing, the culture of secrets lures human agents with the fascination and glory of secrecy.

The two discursive fields are linked where "sensing" and secrecy compensate for the inaccessibility concerning knowledge and comprehension, and hallucinate new forms of participation. The secret cultures describe thereby, though only in part, the state of data politics, in which negotiations and usages of data are done in secret. However, in taking descriptions of symptoms as a starting point, in a similar way to the techno-ecologies, appointing these to the status quo, they run the risk of coagulating into a mode of governmentality. Because the digital arcana legitimizes not only secret policies—which can only be obeyed and followed, but no longer understood, or be actively created by human agents—but also the sealing off of technology with the theoretical model of non-knowing. If non-knowing is the status quo, then all efforts to uncover the secrets within would be in vain.

The dispositif of technospheres that arises from the different discourses thus aims for human agents that are swinging with the technological environment and celebrating self-optimization in sensing. In doing so, they forget the politics of the technospheres. The obedience of this technological being in spheres thereby arises as the new ritual of the political public in digital cultures of mystery.

Ambivalence: Balancing Act between New Descriptions and Politics

The thesis is that on the one hand, in the developing discourse landscape and the dispositif of technospheres, a necessary new description of culture in the time of technological self-organization is being dealt with. On the other hand, it is essential to explore the possibilities of theory formation in the context of the no longer completely understandable and increasingly closed-off technological environments. The problem with this dispositif is that the new ontologies simultaneously, as described, carry politics within themselves that are necessary to be recognized and reflected. The interest in affects and sensitive materiality comes, e.g., out of the fact that with focusing these aspects, more and more dimensions of human agents could be captured and formalized. The captured results of these processes are then firstly transferred to the data economy, as for profiling, and secondly used for the regulation of algorithmically controlled processes. The more users do things, even mistakenly, the more algorithms could "learn." What is celebrated as, for example, new knowledge in the preconscious, world-connectedness of the body, is always usable for economic advantages, too. It is essential, therefore, to examine the current discourse landscape according to its reference to a "regime of affects" (Angerer 2007), co-opting human agents unquestioningly, extensively, and pervasively. They are so enchanted with this (Sprenger 2016) that the concealed modes of data collection and analysis, as well as the interests of major players (Amazon, Google, Facebook), are happily supported. A continuous data supply, consumed in ignorance of its politics, would thus be the meaning and purpose of participation in technological environments.

In this light, non-knowledge and incomprehensibility are important elements in a history of fascination, which the

dispositif of technospheres must be read as. In it, non-knowledge
and incomprehensibility serve to blind and distract human
agents. In such a way, the epistemology after the hermeneutic
mutates to a politics and a regime of non-knowledge and
incomprehensibility.

The great challenge is now to develop new descriptions, what is
absolutely required by the constitution of digital cultures, without
overlooking their politics and governmental aspects. In digital
cultures now, according to the hypotheses, the starting point is
a non-resolvable simultaneity of these two processes, so that
an unceasing balancing act between ontological description and
reflection will be necessary.

With that in mind, the task is therefore to consult and make the
new descriptions readable as discourse and still reveal their
potential for an understanding of, and a way of dealing with,
digital cultures. So how could the technological affecting of smart
things on people be described? How could the technological
environments be seen, without overlooking the demand for
totality (Engemann and Sprenger 2015b, 58) that they and the
discourses of the weak ontologies carry with them? These
undertakings must—and this is the great challenge—occur under
the premise that comprehension and knowledge are hampered,
perhaps forever lost, because of technical blackboxing, the
entanglement in digital cultures, and the interlinking between
method and discovery (Pias 2015). At issue, therefore, is critique in
digital cultures that is concerned with technologically induced, yet
discursively produced, non-knowing and incomprehensibility.

How to Do Critique? Performing Discourses and Technology in Exhibiting Dysfunctional Things

To carry out analysis and reflection, a form of examination
is required that allows, under the discursively generated

situation for knowledge and critique, a reflective distance and at the same time takes into account that there is neither a stable "beyond digital cultures," nor the possibility of under-standing in the traditional hermeneutic sense. What critique under these conditions could look like is to be elucidated in the exhibition-performance "Dysfunctional Things" (*Versehrte Dinge*), which originated at Leuphana University in Lüneburg with students from different programs of study under the banner "complementary studies" in the winter semester 2015/16. The departure point for the project was the following consideration: our technological situation is, it is said, determined by the fact that we and our smart technical things (e.g., smartphones, tablets, fridges, blenders, fitness trackers, and GPS watches), which often know more about us than we do ourselves, live in a symmetric agency. If things and technological environments (such as traffic systems, smart cities, shopping centers) now have their own rights and capacity to act, can we then, for example, simply dispose of those that are malfunctioning? If that is now inappropriate, what would it mean for humans to be surrounded by dysfunctional technical things? These issues were carried by concerns about illuminating the current discourse landscape of digital cultures with the help of exaggerated affirmation of their theoretical description. By doing so the constitution and the effects of non-knowledge and incomprehensibility should also be experienced.

The Exhibition[8]

To explore these questions, an "Owlglass (Till Eulenspiegel) prank," or the art, according to Bazon Brock, of the affirmative word-taken-literally (Brock 1986, 288), was conducted. At the center stood the exaggerated affirmation of and identification with the equality of things and human agents, and the

8   For the complete project documentation, including images, video, and fur-
     ther analysis, see: Leeker 2016.

subsequent dethronement of the latter. The hypothesis was that it is easy to develop theories, but how seriously these theories can be taken can be seen only when they are embodied— because in this process, relevance, consequences, and govern- mentality of theoretical constructs become recognizable when obtained through experience. So the strategy of dealing with and testing the analyzed ambivalent situation of knowledge and critique was to generate theory by acting out discourses as well as technological conditions. Embodying and performing should generate knowledge. This kind of practical forming of theory and knowledge seems also to be adequate in the decen- tralized situation of human agents, as the practices of *acting out* and *embodiment* are always implemented in surroundings and dependent on the indeterminacy of performing, so that there shouldn't be any danger of falling back into ideas of autonomous subjects. The questions for these experiments were: What would cultures look like if the theories mentioned were put into practice? How far will we go in the acceptance of things and our own disempowerment?

To perform this Owlglass prank, the students built or brought malfunctioning things. The things were to have defects, but still be functional. With their dysfunctions, so the thinking goes, they would impose specific behaviors on the human users, which would make visible and palpable how dys/functional things shape humans.

The exhibition and performances with the dysfunctional things raised a veritable parallel world of agency of things and humans. It was like a contemporary science fiction in which what is said has already become everyday culture. A look at the projects is illustrative of this.

[Fig. 1] Exhibition: Dysfunctional Things. Photography: Martina Leeker & Laila Walter, Lüneburg 2016.

Interfaces, through which human agents gain access to technological environments, are important in digital cultures. Interfaces enable not just control of technological operations; they shape, through their design, the behavior of users. They are therefore a sensitive gateway to the technological worlds and models and regimes of human-machine interaction. The exhibition asks what would happen when, assuming a radical equality of things, interfaces are disrupted and cannot be thrown away? In this context, a workstation was created that had a defective computer mouse, which performed self-willed movements enabling the production of strange drawings.

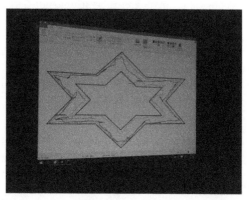

[Fig. 2] Exhibition: Dysfunctional Things. Project: Train your Brain (Jan-Erik Förster). Photography: Martina Leeker & Laila Walter, Lüneburg 2016.

There is a big difference between criticizing an interface for poor user-friendliness, and thoughtfully taking it into account and being glad of disruptions.

[Fig. 3] Exhibition: Dysfunctional Things. Project: Betreuungszentrum für grenzüberschreitende Geräte / Care Center for Cross-Border Devices (Julie Heitmann, Nadine Teichmann, Franziska Debey). Photography: Martina Leeker & Laila Walter, Lüneburg 2016.

The "Betreuungszentrum für grenzüberschreitende Geräte" (BGG) (Care Center for Cross-Border Devices) was another work. Here, dysfunctional things could be put into care so that they wouldn't cause damage left unattended. At the BGG, a completely unique educational and behavioral culture ensued, which ranged from psychological training with device co-operators for appropriate contact with technical things, to new courses in electropedagogy, for example.

In the artificial world of dysfunctional things, the "Market for Dysfunctional Smartphones" marked the station that congenially spelled out the economic side of the new world of things and data. When people can no longer get rid of their smartphones, a peculiar business could be created with their purchase. This business idea was implemented by an ingenious start-up. Owners of dysfunctional smartphones could offer them for purchase to the new company via the Internet. The enterprising business could then accept payment from the former owner to appropriately store the device on their behalf.

[Fig. 4] Exhibition: Dysfunctional Things. Project: Markt für versehrte Smartphones / Market for Dysfunctional Smartphones (Laila Walter). Photography: Martina Leeker, Lüneburg 2016.

As an example of the storage, a dysfunctional smartphone was presented on an altar decked out with lavish offerings like exquisite fruits and flowers.

Data rights have become a very important topic in the world of Owlglass prank in the exhibition, because smart things are technical devices controlled by algorithms collecting and processing data.

[Fig. 5] Exhibition: Dysfunctional Things. Project: Magna Carta der Datenrechte / Magna Charta of Data Rights (Martina Keup). Photography: Martina Leeker & Laila Walter, Lüneburg 2016.

In data rights now, as based on human rights, the right to the protection of life, to freedom of movement, and to assembly (compatibility) have been conceded to data. One consequence of these rights is, for example, that because of freedom of movement human agents should no longer be allowed to use methods of data protection.

The Owlglass Prank as a Method of Critique and Resistance

The exhibition-performance concerns itself with both sides of the current discourse landscape outlined here, namely (1) the discourse of the techno-ecology and (2) the digital mysterium.

One focus was on the forms of non-knowledge and incomprehensibility produced by them, which were affirmed and thereby criticized.

(1) The discourse-on-things and on techno-ecology were taken on seriously and experienced in an exaggerated manner. Non-knowledge and incomprehensibility generated by these discourses, which emerged from the complex agencies and the technological environments, became new possibilities of (non-) knowledge. This knowledge from non-knowledge, and its effects, were clear and concise in the "Kleiderflüsterin" (clothes whisperer). New levels and forms of sensibility were reached by listening to damaged clothes and hearing of their desire for repairs.

[Fig. 6] Exhibition: Dysfunctional Things. Project: Kleiderflüsternde Nähwerkstatt / Clothes Whispering Sewing Room (Nadine Teichmann). Photography: Martina Leeker & Laila Walter, Lüneburg 2016.

It had the effect of, among other things, stitching together the arms of her sweater and so "dysfunctionalising" the wearer's hands. In the exhibition it was, however, immediately clear that

these new forms of knowledge arise from imaginings and—
as with the *Kleiderflüsterin*—could be loaded with animistic
reminiscences.

The Owlglass prank was also an attempt to explore (2) the proclaimed digital mysterium. What was remarkable was that in the
exhibition, the mysterium had already become an integral part
of the dysfunctionally functioning everyday world. A particularly
striking expression of this was the "Declaration of Data Rights
of Things." Because with it, the digital mysterium became, in the
shape of the inviolability of data, the law, and human agents its
co-operative partners.

In the examination of both discourses, exaggerated affirmation
was the trigger for critical reflection. Through the performers and
the visitors entering the discursive landscapes, affirming them
and living them, their critical, political, or governmental aspects
could light up—so the performing of exaggeration produced its
own theoretical input.

Knowledge of Tricksters

The exhibition had the task of enabling, through exaggerated
affirmation and performance, a discourse analysis of digital
cultures in periods of impeded or thwarted hermeneutics. It was
crucial to produce embodiment and performance as an epistemological device that could generate and train the ambivalent
thinking described here, which correlates with a balancing act
between description and analysis. To do this, the performers
acted as "tricksters." This hybrid figure was of interest because
tricksters, according to Erhard Schüttpelz (2010), not only disrupt
the consensus but above all provoke conflicting interpretations
and ensnare those affected in an unresolvable contrariness. A
thing is not simply either good or bad, but always both and, furthermore, a third thing in which contradictions are conveyed as
not mediative.

This status of the trickster thus corresponds to the previously mentioned constitution of digital cultures. New descriptions of the "situation" are in fact necessary and yet they have to be checked constantly according to their discursive, political and governmental effects, and potential. In this situation, the trickster and the thinking that he provokes can be considered an appropriate epistemological stance and exercise for digital cultures—because they set up permanent, cognitive-affective multi-stable figures with which various kinds of re-thinking can be activated and supported.

In this way, digital cultures get into a state of liminality (Schüttpelz 2010) via tricksters, a transience that never ends and will not culminate in any new order. The trickstery becomes thus a form of action and thinking that could influence digital cultures by intervening in ontologization with exaggerated affirmation and contradictions.

How to go on? Practice of Critique in Digital Cultures

The reflective level and the standpoint of critique presented in the "Dysfunctional Things" project thus appeared to both performers and visitors as an embodiment and experience of theoretic visions and discourses as well as technological conditions. That is to say, theory and conditions should become reflectable in action, so that the positions of critique in the "artificial worlds" arose from those worlds and their behavior within them. A "critique from aesthetic experience" and secondly an "aesthetic experience of critique" were enabled through the embodiment of theories in the exhibition in this way.

This "practice of critique" responds to the constitution of the discursively and technologically generated state of knowledge, research, and critique in digital cultures, which, as mentioned, are being confronted with the dictum of non-knowledge,

incomprehensibility, pre-conscious sensing, and with continuous
self/reflection and the simultaneity of new ontological description
and critical analysis. Furthermore, digital cultures are constituted
of ubiquitous infrastructures that form technological environments impossible to escape. The upshot of this is that critique
lies in the discourses surrounding it and in the situation that is
generated by the former, no longer positioned "outside," which
was, to date, considered essential. Instead of stepping outside
of techno-cultural conditions, in the project a stepping into them
was experimented with, which should make it possible to find
a position of critique in the interior. This interior does not refer
to the position of a subject. The exaggerated identification that
makes things and human agents unfamiliar gives rise instead to
an "inner as outer" and an "outer as inner." In this configuration,
it is about critique in and out of the entanglement with the
surrounding environment. And it is to deal in a productive way
with non-knowledge.

After Criticism: Smuggling, Looking Away (Irit Rogoff), and Performing

The "practice of critique" can be further defined as a method
of reflection for digital cultures because it goes far beyond
traditional forms of criticism, which became inefficient with the
crisis of hermeneutics, and opposes vehemently any form of
"criticism" (Rogoff 2003). Criticism, according to Irit Rogoff, was
based on recognition and understanding, as it intended to make
the invisible visible, condemn in- and exclusion, and denounce
injustices.[9] In place of this concept and practice of criticism,
Rogoff puts "criticality" (2003). The point of departure for this
concept is that one cannot stand outside of the situation that one

9   For the "embodiment of critique" it is therefore necessary to move away
     from the criticism of judging and valuating, just as Michel Foucault has called
     for with suspending judgment (Sprenger 2014). Judging criticism must in fact
     be seen as its own discourse and separate regime because it makes claims
     to a sovereignty of interpretation (Rogoff 2003).

is criticizing. In digital cultures, a similar situation results from the interwovenness of methods, technologies, and discourses (on digital cultures as well as on critique) in which little exists beyond the digital. According to Rogoff, it is an "inhabitation of a condition in which we are deeply embedded as well as being critically conscious" (2006, 5). Even if it is presupposed in the text that the concepts of critique are also generated discursively, as, for example, the present-day loss of distance, and become real in this constitution, the ideas of Rogoff are of interest to follow-up methods of dealing with the emerged contemporary situation of the loss of distance. Rogoff proposes two methods with which this "inhabitation" could be realized. They could be tested for their value and also for the reflection and formation of theory in the technological and discursive conditions of digital cultures.

Rogoff sees "smuggling" (2006) as a method to fulfill infiltration in established and legitimate order. Smuggling moves along borders and breaks through spots that are permeable. The goal of smuggling is not resistance or destruction, but existing in a different order in an established situation. In this constitution, smuggling is a quasi-part of the existing law and order and at the same time a method of their reflection.

To smuggling belongs "looking away" (Rogoff 2005). Looking away turns from an anti-hermeneutic impulse against "thorough inspection" that is bound up with the idea that preexisting meanings lying under the surface could be seen. Looking away, in contrast, would bring strange and unexpected events into existence and meaning would be vacant and fluid. Looking away is a way of participating in cultures, because with this method and attitude the power of discourse is questioned and other voices are heard. With regard to the proclaimed digital arcana, the voices of the excluded could be kept present before its gates with aesthetic displacements.

The method of "performances of the Owlglass prank" could be added to the two other previously mentioned methods, as it had

been tested in the exhibition. Rather than the sensing and being
shrouded in secrecy of the digital mysterium, the pranks employ
the in/security and unpredictability of performance, with which
an entirely different analysis of the power discourse could be
formed. These allow the hermetic facades of the cultures of non-
knowing and incomprehensibility to be permeable, and produce
insights into their discursive constitution and "politics."

In/Forming Cultures: Inventing Alien Worlds

What was tested in the project "Dysfunctional Things" as a
method of intervening in the current discourses of the constitution of digital cultures and critique shall be considered further in conclusion. The question is how a concrete displacement
in the discourse field of digital cultures and in the dispositif
of technospheres could come about. It is above all a matter
of allowing a different world view, and to imagine and realize
different orders via these displacements.

Fundamentally, "unlearning" (Sternfeld 2014) is essential for
the formation of different cultures. But what has been learned
cannot simply be forgotten, because it is embedded deeply in
body and behavior. That is, the production of non-knowledge and
incomprehensibility is at stake. This does not happen, however,
in the context of a regime of secrecy or techno-ecology, but in
the sense of experimentation with the thresholds of knowledge
and non-knowledge. At stake here is the enabling of the re-
appropriation and displacement of what is sayable, visible, and
interpretable.

These forms and methods of productive critique can be
integrated within the concept of "in/forming cultures." This is
proposed as a contribution to critique in the specific, technological, epistemological, and discursive conditions of digital
cultures outlined here. What is meant by this is that (a) a sep-
arate, artificial, e.g., excessive, strange, and unfamiliar, culture is
created, performed, and made accessible. This culture formation

(b) "in/forms" existing cultures in terms of their education by reflecting them. From this double formation arises (c) in small scope, meaning local, temporary, case-specific displacements in the see- and say-able. From these, in turn, other stories and collective action spaces of self-empowerment may arise. This refers to the production of artificial and parallel worlds in which unfamiliar ways of living or unknown technological structures operate. They follow their own logic, with which they continuously infiltrate the dominant cultures. These parallel worlds would, therefore, on one hand expose the contra-factuality of existing cultures with the owlglassy exaggerated affirmation. On the other hand, they would survey and test as artificial worlds, for example, technological possibilities or other forms of life for their potential. It is entirely a matter of repeated questioning, reconsidering, and rethinking of the non-knowledge and incomprehensibility in digital cultures, in order to open and colonize a space of reflection and knowledge between technology and discursively produced non-knowledge. Much could, in fact, be quite different because—as set forth here—digital cultures are in large part created discursively and as such are politically useful.

Thank you to the students of the "Dysfunctional Things" seminar for their projects.

References

Angerer, Marie-Luise. 2007. *Vom Begehren nach dem Affekt*. Zürich/Berlin: Diaphanes.

Barad, Karen. 2003. "Posthumanist Performativity: Toward an Understanding of How Matter Comes to Matter." *Signs: Journal of Women in Culture and Society* 28 (3): 801–831.

Beyes, Timon, and Claus Pias. 2014. "Debatte: Transparenz und Geheimnis." *Zeitschrift für Kulturwissenschaft* 2: 111–118.

Brock, Bazon. 1986. "Aller gefährlicher Unsinn entsteht aus dem Kampf gegen die Narren, oder Eulenspiegel als Philosoph, Nietzsche als sein gelehrigster Schüler und der Avantgardist als Hofnarr der Gesellschaft." In *Ästhetik gegen erzwungene Unmittelbarkeit. Die Gottsucherbande – Schriften 1978–1986*, edited by Bazon Brock, 288–292. Köln: Dumont.

Derrida, Jacques, and Hans-Georg Gadamer. 2004. *Der ununterbrochene Dialog*. Frankfurt am Main: Suhrkamp.

Engemann, Christoph, and Florian Sprenger, eds. 2015a. *Internet der Dinge. Über smarte Objekte, intelligente Umgebungen und die technische Durchdringung der Welt*. Bielefeld: transcript.

Engemann, Christoph, and Florian Sprenger. 2015b. "Im Netz der Dinge. Zur Einleitung." In *Internet der Dinge. Über smarte Objekte, intelligente Umgebungen und die technische Durchdringung der Welt*, edited by Christoph Engemann, and Florian Sprenger, 7–58. Bielefeld: transcript.

Foucault, Michel. 1994. *Überwachen und Strafen: Die Geburt des Gefängnisses*. Frankfurt am Main: Suhrkamp. (Original French edition: *Surveiller et punir – la naissance de la prison*, Paris: Gallimard 1975.)

Galloway, Alexander. 2011. "Are Some Things Unrepresentable?" *Theory, Culture & Society* 28 (7/8): 85–102.

Hansen, Mark B. N. 2011. "Medien des 21. Jahrhunderts, technisches Empfinden und unsere originäre Umweltbedingung." In *Die technologische Bedingung. Beiträge zur Beschreibung der technischen Welt*, edited by Erich Hörl, 365–409. Berlin: Suhrkamp.

Hörl, Erich, ed. 2011. *Die technologische Bedingung. Beiträge zur Beschreibung der technischen Welt*. Berlin: Suhrkamp.

Hörl, Erich. 2014. "Die technologische Sinnverschiebung. Orte des Unermesslichen." In *Orte des Unermesslichen. Theater nach der Geschichtsteleologie*, edited by Marita Tatari, 43–63. Zürich/Berlin: diaphanes.

Hörl, Erich. 2016. "Other Beginnings of Participative Sense Culture: Wild Media, Speculative Ecologies, Transgressions of the Cybernetic Hypothesis." In *ReClaiming Participation: Technology, Mediation, Collectivity*, edited by Mathias Denecke, Anne Ganzert, Isabell Otto, and Robert Stock, 91–119. Bielefeld: transcript.

Kittler, Friedrich. 1986. *Grammophon, Film, Typewriter*. Berlin: Brinkman & Bose.

Latour, Bruno, and Peter Weibel, eds. 2005. *Making Things Public: Atmospheres of Democracy*. Cambridge, MA: MIT Press.

Latour, Bruno. 2008. *Wir sind nie modern gewesen*. Frankfurt am Main: Suhrkamp.

Latour, Bruno. 2010. "An Attempt at a 'Compositionist Manifesto.'" *New Literary History* 41 (3): 471–490.

Latour, Bruno. 2013. "The Anthropocene and the Destruction of the Image of the Globe." *Gifford Lecture Series: Facing Gaia – A New Enquiry into Natural Religion* (4th Gifford Lecture). Accessed February 26, 2017. https://www.youtube.com/watch?v=4-l6FQN4P1c.

Leeker, Martina. 2016. "Versehrte Dinge: Eine Ausstellungs-Performance im Übergang zum Technosphärischen." *Experiments&Interventions: Diskursanalytische Ästhetiken für digitale Kulturen*. Accessed February 28, 2017. http://projects.digital-cultures.net/dcrl-experiments-interventions/environments-und-infrastrukturen/versehrte-dinge.

Luhmann, Niklas. 2001. "Was ist Kommunikation." In *Aufsätze und Reden*, edited by Oliver Jahraus, 94–110. Stuttgart: Reclam.

McLuhan, Marshall. 1964. *Understanding Media: The Extensions of Man*. New York: McGraw-Hill.

78   Pias, Claus. 2015. "Nicht-Verstehen in Digitalen Kulturen." Vortrag auf der
          Hyperkult XXV. Accessed July 20, 2016. http://avmstream.leuphana.de/
          claus-pias-nicht-verstehen-in-digitalen-kulturen.

Pias, Claus. 2016. "Collectives, Connectives, and the 'Nonsense' of Participation."
          In *ReClaiming Participation: Technology, Mediation, Collectivity*, edited by Mathias
          Denecke, Anne Ganzert, Isabell Otto, and Robert Stock, 23–38. Bielefeld:
          transcript.

Rogoff, Irit. 2003. "Vom Kritizismus über die Kritik zur Kritikalität" *Webjournal
          European Institute for Progressive Cultural Policies*. Accessed July 20, 2016. http://
          eipcp.net/transversal/0806/rogoff1/de.

Rogoff, Irit. 2005. "Looking Away: Participations in Visual Culture." In *After Criticism:
          New Responses to Art and Performance*, edited by Gavin Butt, 117–134. Oxford:
          Blackwell Publishing.

Rogoff, Irit. 2006. "'Smuggling' – An Embodied Criticality." *Webjournal European
          Institute for Progressive Cultural Policies*. Accessed July 20, 2016. http://eipcp.net/
          dlfiles/rogoff-smuggling.

Schüttpelz, Erhard. 2010. "Der Trickster." In *Die Figur des Dritten: Ein kulturwissen-
          schaftliches Paradigma*, edited by Eva Eßlinger, Tobias Schlechtriemen, Doris
          Schweitzer, and Alexander Zons, 208–224. Berlin: Suhrkamp.

Sprenger, Florian. 2014. "Die Kontingenz des Gegebenen: Zur Zeit der Datenkritik."
          Mediale Kontrolle unter Beobachtung 3 (1). Accessed July 20, 2016. http://www.
          medialekontrolle.de/wp-content/uploads/2014/09/Sprenger-Florian-2014-03-01.
          pdf.

Sprenger, Florian. 2016. "Handlungsmächte und Zauberei ohne Zauberer – Von
          der Beseelung der Dinge zum Ubiquitous Computing." In *Trick 17*, edited by Jan
          Müggenburg, and Sebastian Vehlken, 87–114. Lüneburg: meson press. http://
          meson.press/wp-content/uploads/2016/06/9783957960818_Trick_17.pdf.

Sternfeld, Nora. 2014. "Verlernen vermitteln." *Kunstpädagogische Positionen* 30.
          Accessed July 20, 2016. http://kunst.uni-koeln.de/kpp/_kpp_daten/pdf/KPP30_
          Sternfeld.pdf.

Vehlken, Sebastian. 2016. "What are digital cultures?" *DCRL Questions—Research
          Interviews*. Accessed February 26, 2017. https://vimeo.com/182711911.

IN/TRANSPARENCY

POLITICS OF KNOWLEDGE

AUTHORITIES/EXPERTS

(DIGITAL) GATEKEEPERS

NARRATOR

EPISTEMOLOGY OF MISTRUST

THE CIRCLE

[5]

On the Side of Non-Knowledge: Mistrust. Heinrich von Kleist's *The Duel* on Big Data Curation

Jeannie Moser

This paper historicizes the ambivalent discourse on data and communication transparency that is epidemic in digital cultures by confronting it with a reading of Kleist's novella, *The Duel* (1811). In the medium of literature, conditions of possibility for the production of relevant and reliable knowledge on the basis of data are subject to analysis and critique. Basic operations of data processing have proven to be fallible and corrupted by media, which, instead of reducing complexity, deepen it. In contradistinction to the trust that reduces this complexity, *The Duel* performs an epistemology of mistrust, which insists on the polyvalence, dubiousness, agility, and ephemerality of the data from which truth is supposed to appear.

Intro: Dystopic Transparency

Literature contributes to, shares, intensifies, radicalizes, and, sometimes, exaggerates current discourses and ideas. Regarding the latter, in Dave Eggers' dystopic novel *The Circle,* computer systems collect, exchange, and provide such unbelievable quantities of information that all gaps in non-knowledge seem to be eliminated irrevocably. The novel relates a hip and fancy Silicon Valley culture fully saturated with digital technologies, which augur the disclosure, communication, and monitoring of simply everything, by everyone. It is a culture that absolutely refuses to admit the opaque, the withheld, the ambivalent, the incomprehensible, or the overlooked. Because each of those impermanent and negotiable non-knowledge derivatives indicates an utter insufficiency, the primary rule in this culture is: *all that happens must be known. Secrets are lies, sharing is caring,* and *privacy is theft* are the corresponding slogans of the gigantic Circle Corporation, which has centralized all services provided by Google, Facebook, Twitter, Apple, etc. into a media concept called TruYou.

In *The Circle*, political governance, the governance of the self, and the governance of data all intermingle to form a highly sensitive alliance. Power structures are refaced in a radical way— ostensibly as the ideal of transparency reverts into a tyranny of the visible. Both private individuals and public figures start to wear cameras, which transmit a 24/7 feed that can be followed and commented on by the whole net community. Surveillance gets democratized. Political and computer programs intersect in a software program called Demoxie that is supposed to facilitate

the most pure and direct democracy, a "democracy with *your*
voice, and *your* moxie" (Eggers 2013, 396).

Big Data, Agency, and the Specter of Non-Knowledge

The Circle is an intensification of the present, as dystopias
are in general. It strongly resembles open source tools like
LiquidFeedback, which powers Internet platforms for proposition
development and decision-making by "heeding the voice of
constituencies on a permanent basis, feeding it back directly
to political processes at hand" (Hendriks 2014). But, most
notably, it amplifies a discourse that claims ignorance is irrevocably something in need of correction (Proctor 2008, 2), and
that everything one needs for such correction is freely available
on the Internet. The masses of data that abound in a fluidized
archive promise omniscience (Stalder 2015) and link omniscience
to omnipotence: everyone will have the ability to become an
autonomous and sovereign expert who detects the truth.

What this discourse ignores, however, is that accessibility, transparency, and truth are not actually identical. An accumulation
of information alone does not produce truth. The direction is
missing, the singular and binding meaning, namely, that which
is reliant on distinctions (Han 2013, 17; Proctor 2008, 3). This is
what Raymond Geuss, in his commentary on Jacques de Saint
Victor's *The Anti-Political*, correspondingly uses to counter
demands for a direct Web 2.0 participatory democracy run by,
for instance, pirate parties all over the world. In the 2015 book,
the discussion concerns Western democracies of mistrust, which
are marked by the querulousness of their politics. Its point of
departure is the observation that individuals and movements
who understand themselves as anti-political and who demand
that the corrupt, opaque authorities and experts all abdicate
are being increasingly affirmed, driven by an idea that lends
itself to paranoia: that authorities and experts "actively work to

organize doubt or uncertainty or misinformation to help maintain ignorance" (Proctor 2008, 8).

Criticism and even skepticism of Geuss and de Saint Victor are directed at answers offered by the anti-political, which rest on a digitalization of politics. They are also directed at the phantasm of total transparency, which, purportedly, enables independent formation of opinions, judgment, and agency—conceptualized as being beyond the established, mistrusted critical faculties, brain trusts, representative instances, and institutions of power that control the flow of information (de Saint Victor and Geuss 2015). In fact, power is concentrated in the ordering of data. Early modern political theory had already noticed that the essence of power lies in the government of channels through which information passes (Vogl 2010). Agency condenses in filters that direct the data flow by supposing and separating the relevant and the irrelevant, dividing knowledge and non-knowledge from each other.

But, according to Geuss, the problem is not with the structure of (political) institutions, although they organize data, rather it is that political systems are always embedded in economic orders— the blind spot of the anti-political. And from there it isn't far to the much-praised transparency. Google's algorithms dictate the boundaries of knowledge: "What one can know is the content of an *average* Google search," Geuss writes, "a nearly unending flood of irrelevant facts, lies, speculative fantasies, half- and quarter-truths, misleading insinuations, and completely uncontrolled expressions of opinions" (2015, 105f.; Stalder 2015).

Still, even more fundamental and severe is the procedure itself, which grinds out the status of both knowledge and non-knowledge. That status remains a matter requiring continuous negotiation. The borders between their areas of efficacy and legitimacy must be redrawn incessantly. And, for the most part, knowledge and non-knowledge are contaminated, calling for spaces of transition (Bies and Gamper 2012). Seen in this light,

the dream of total knowledge and the specter of ignorance are
equally bound to digital technologies. But that is something not
actually specific to digital culture's new electronic media:

> the ubiquity of the Internet, the increasing monopolization
> of the flow of data by companies like Google and Microsoft
> and the nearly incomprehensible bulk of information (of
> completely unclear epistemic value) depict at best the
> intensification of an already problematic epistemic crisis situ-
> ation. (Geuss 2015, 107)

Epistemic Crisis

Knowledge, as digital technologies are providing it, discursively
figures as a cache of electronically preserved and accessible
data. But it is still confronted with the dilemma produced by the
steady urgency of ordering, evaluating, and structuring these
confusing masses of data. A persistent difficulty is segregating
the meaningful from the meaningless, and thereby establishing
the difference between knowledge and non-knowledge—that
is what has precipitated the epistemic crisis. So even if digital
cultures consider themselves as having escaped from the realm
of non-knowledge, access to data doesn't suffice. Effective agency
depends on the mutability of individual data points. It depends
on the ability to recognize the relevant connections—in other
words, on complex and extremely critical processing procedures
worth a closer look.

The diagnosis of an intensifying epistemic crisis attending big
data means, from a historical perspective, that the crisis is of
longue durée; the threshold had appeared by 1800 at the latest.
Since then, the question of the conditions of possibility and the
boundaries of knowledge has been pressing, and boils down to
the paradoxical conclusion: "knowledge of one's ignorance is a
precondition for enlightenment" (Proctor 2008, 5). The question
arises because knowledge is no longer merely collected. The
problem of the production, storage, and transmission of data

produced by the state, by people, by science, by nature, and by economics arises. How can it be curated? What is relevant to the contemporary situation? From around 1800, knowledge branches out into forms of organization and administration intended to make data operable. Gaps between the multiplicity of things, contingent masses of data and ordering principals, between the state and the individual that produce spaces of non-knowledge, are asking to be closed (Schäffner 1999).

Coevally, by no means at all, is it extraordinary to dream the dream of transparency, to state that appearances are deceiving or to press charges against (aristocratic) camouflage and dissimulation. The terms that are seeing inflationary usage and concern are: to debunk, disclose, publicize and expose (Starobinski 1988, 12; Schneider 2013).

Heinrich von Kleist's *The Duel*

It was during this historic state of epistemic crisis that Heinrich von Kleist wrote novellas, plays, newspaper articles, and numerous private letters by hand. Notwithstanding his analogous reference system, it is Kleist to whom current media theory owes insights into procedures of data curation, the challenging and awkward practices and techniques that are essential to the conversion of vast reams of data into relevant knowledge, and in turn, to the restriction of non-knowledge. Uniquely, all of his writings reflect and examine the very same epistemic system transformations that have been gaining momentum since 1800— linking them to a fundamental media critique.

Describing transmission, perception, administration, and management of information almost obsessively, his writings process—even in the mode of presentation itself—the ways in which knowledge is subject to media. In his writings, an issue is made of the fact that media increase complexity rather than reduce it. In whatever form, communication is attended by random noise. Kleist's texts perform failures, misinterpretations, overhasty and lazy conclusions. They highlight the disability **87**

and oppression that escort enlightenment's optimistic claims
to universality. In turn, the equality and honesty of sources and
information providers hang in the balance. Determining truth is
always a risky operation full of vulnerabilities. And the invis-
ibleness of power technologies remains.

The novella *The Duel* appeared in print in 1811. The author,
corresponding to a world of analogous media, dislocates us,
thrusting us into a world not even acquainted with the printing
press. He displaces us into a world organized by neither republic
nor democratic principles.

The Duel begins with the depiction of a murder that occurs at
the end of the 14th century. The Duke of Breysach, who has just
effected the legitimation of a son born out of wedlock as the heir
to the throne, is shot by an arrow. His half-brother, Jacob Rotbart,
with whom he had lived in a state of feud, is under suspicion for
being the owner of the arrow and having been absent at the time
of the offense. But Rotbart claims, in front of the court, that he
spent the night with Littegarde von Auerstein, who, according
to the narrator, *one must know* had "until the utterance of this
scandalous slur, enjoyed the purest and most blameless of rep-
utations" (293).[1] As evidence, he presents a ring that he received
as a parting gift from Littegarde, and, in turn, raises charges
against her. Littegarde's father, Winfried von Breda, receives
the scandalous notification concerning his daughter and, upon
reading the court's "terrible communication," he is immediately
seized by apoplexy (294f.). Littegarde is subsequently cast out of
the house of Breda by her brothers, which leads to dissent concerning the inheritance after the death of the patriarch.

Only Friedrich von Trota, the chamberlain of the murdered Duke
of Breysach, is convinced of Littegarde's innocence. Assured of

1   References to *The Duel* translated by David Luke and Nigel Reeves (1978)
     are only indicated with page numbers. Paraphrases refer to *Der Zweikampf*
     (1994).

the falsity of Rotbart's testimony, the chamberlain challenges Rotbart to a holy duel. During this ordeal, which subjected the defendant to a game of strict rules, a struggle with his own body (Foucault 2002, 712), Friedrich is, curiously, badly injured. The injury is seen as the end of the fight, so trumpets sound a threefold flourish and Rotbart sets "his foot on the fallen knight's breast" (306). Friedrich and Littegarde are sentenced to death due to sinful invocation of divine judgment. But then the story, due to a "strange and remarkable fact," takes an "unexpected turn of events" (313f.), which, considering Kleist, is not actually all that unexpected.

The Truth Mediated by Evidence and Ordeal

The story makes an effort to illuminate multiple cases that are tightly interlocked. Criminal guilt, deception, virtue, and honor come into play. But the story is much more about the reconstruction, or simply the construction, of that which is not known. It concerns an agitation in the gray area between knowledge and ignorance, which simultaneously grasps the store of secured knowledge and, on the other hand, reaches out towards that which cannot or cannot yet be known—in other words, towards procedures and practices of investigation. And those are linked to epistemic media.

Both earthly and divine courts are convened, and throughout the story, things are inspected, and papers are shipped—inquiries, letters, and fragments of documents and files. These are read, or, more exactly, often over-read, and then evidence is presented, witnesses are called and investigated, private conversations are conducted as interrogations, statements are collected, and, finally, everything is interpreted. It can therefore be said of *The Duel* that it takes the conditions of possibility for the production of relevant and reliable knowledge on the basis of data as the focal point of its reflections. Exploiting the register of transparency, it forces the question about that which actually is to reveal or to pervade—and furthermore it asks whether the disclosed, if it were there, would even be recognized or would, in contrast, be overlooked several times (cf. Claus Pias' and Timon Beyes' contribution to this volume).

Lacking a thrilling plot or an ingenious investigator figure, and instead coming up with abrupt shifts in perspective, curious and implausible changes of characters, of lines of action, as well as of topics, the novella mainly addresses data curation operations themselves. The medium of literature turns into a program of observation of non-knowledge and its administration. At the core of the novella is the question of how, or whether it is even possible that something can be taken from a confusing collection of contingencies and be identified as significant—touching on the very difference between the availability and the classifiability of data. The boundaries to which it leads are the boundaries of certainty—namely, beyond the inquisitorial means of truth deter-mination (Bergengruen 2011, 135).

On the one hand, the story takes us into a medievally tinted version of a debate about reasoning on the basis of evidence as it was established in the eighteenth century. It sets forensic practice as a philological-hermeneutical method of reading written and spoken signs, things and facts into motion, all of which, however, are staged as liminal phenomena and are equipped with an index of illegibility. On the other hand, divine judgment is supposed to decide the dispute through supernatural signs. It is God who shall safeguard communication against bias, disaccord, and dubiety (Hahn 2008, 286). Hence, the text, we can say with Roland Reuß, depicts the duel less in the context of the question of justice than in the context of the contentious core of truth.

The sacred verdict of arms in the holy duel—which, strictly speaking, is a binary-structured game that determines victory or defeat (Foucault 2002, 713)—is supposed to determine truth in a legal dispute and should, infallibly, bring that truth to light (303). The truth is therefore not entirely independent of the question of what the fighting subjects hold to be true. But the gap between the desired manifestation of truth and the subject-bound claims of truthfulness in Kleist's texts is depicted as irresolvable (Reuß 1994, 8f.).

If God's word is supposed to adjudicate on Rotbart's statement, or as it says in the story, to decide "the truth of the testimony against [Littegarde] to which he has sworn," (303) it is actually completely unambiguous and transparent. But neither the spectators of the duel nor the readers of *The Duel* are capable of knowing that in the moment. Which is why and where the story takes its surprising turn: an "apparently insignificant" scratch (314) that Rotbart sustains develops into a lethal wound, whereas the defeated Trota returns to flourishing health and demands that the battle continue. The text, therefore, produces differing opinions about the proper method of reading God's message, if not about its fundamental legibility: "What mortal man," Trota asks, "could presume to interpret the mysterious verdict God has delivered in this duel?" (307). The text unites the evidence and the institution of the duel by turning it, in equal measure, into an uncertain matter of interpretation, an erratic question of analysis and negotiation. Their maximal epistemic resilience is subject to rigorous testing.

Trust as the Radiant Hero of the Story

Contemporary evidence, as well as the anachronistic trial by ordeal (it had already disappeared from European juridical life in the twelfth and thirteenth centuries), proves unreliable. It is, instead, demonstrated to be in need of interpretation and therefore subject to erroneous human imputations. Both are, therefore, associated with a non-juridical option. The story introduces another entity, which seems to unlock a direct and immediate path to the truth: Kleist makes trust into the radiant hero of his story, personified in the figure of Friedrich von Trota, the glowing advocate of Littegarde's innocence. This corresponds to the discursive condensation through which trust reveals itself as imperial, and which, like the threshold of the epistemic crisis, is datable to 1800: the trusting and trustworthy person as a subject of agency enters into the limelight.[2] Mistrust, in turn, is discredited and arrives only as a specter.

When Littegarde's brothers, who are busy speculating about their inheritance, cast her out, she turns to Trota for help. When she tells him what happened, he interrupts her:

> Say no more … There is a voice that speaks for you in my heart, and it carries a far livelier conviction than any assurances, indeed than all the evidence and proofs which the combination of events and circumstances may well enable you to bring in your favor before the court at Basle. (299)

To demonstrate her irreproachability, Trota tenders himself to Littegarde as an attorney of trust, who, through a combination of thought and unwavering feeling, of knowledge and faith, expects certainty. The case becomes an anti-juridical matter of the heart, which demands a pledge to the law of the heart. As trust shows as a gap in communication, which demands a leap in the dark that may have fatal consequences, and, at the same time, has to be made out of communication (Hahn 2008, 229), the voice of the heart competes against the language of the ambivalent pieces of evidence and of text. Feelings and morality are placed in opposition to reflection, appearances, criminalistic logic, and against "arbitrary human laws" (308), such as those that determine that a fight is at its end at the statement of a judge and cannot begin again. With Anne Fleig following Niklas Luhmann, trust is placed at the center of the story as an unconditional trust. It becomes a risky advanced payment, performed as a practice. Trust gambles itself, and the stakes are high—divine judgment risks a battle of life and death (Fleig 2013, 98).

---

2   For the wide-ranging research literature cf. exemplarily Fleig 2013; Frevert 2003 and 2013; Hardin 2004 and 2006; Hartmann 2011; Luhmann 2009; and Reemtsma 2008.

Trust encounters difficult-to-judge information by abridging the gap and translating non-knowledge (once it acquired a professed form) directly into action even where there is no transparency (Han 2013, 78f.). Its discursive antagonist, mistrust, on the other hand, is an opposite posture towards an abundance of data of entirely uncertain epistemic value. Precisely by keeping the gap between knowledge and non-knowledge open and broadening it by strong imaginations, it becomes productive and might agitate critically. Quite remarkably, though *The Duel* is a text in which trust makes a fulminant appearance, it also performs this options and possibilities augmenting specter posture in parallel.

The Mistrust of the Emperor

Unlike trust, mistrust does not at first glance appear to figure in *The Duel*. The character from which it proceeds receives little space to reveal or define himself. It is the emperor. He enters the action in his function as the bearer of power without being at all fleshed out in either a psychological or a narrative sense. Nevertheless (or therefore) insights into the function and the operational mode of mistrust can be adduced. There is one passage where mistrust appears explicitly, and it is not just *any* passage, but an extremely sensitive moment: precisely where both the process of converting the unknowable and the narrative take an unexpected turn. Trota and Littegarde are condemned to an ignominious death by fire, and the sentence:

> would have been carried out at once, ... if it had not been the Emperor's secret intention that Count Jakob Rotbart, against whom he could not suppress a certain feeling of mistrust, should be present at the execution. But the strange and remarkable fact was that Count Jakob still lay sick of the small and apparently insignificant wound which Herr Friedrich had inflicted on him ... and all of the skill of the doctors ... could not avail to close it. Indeed, a corrosive discharge of a kind quite unknown to the medical science of those days, began

to spread through the whole structure of his hand, eating it
away like a cancer right down to the bone; in consequence,
..., it had become necessary to amputate the entire diseased
hand, and later, ... his entire arm. But this too, ... merely had
the effect of, as could easily have been foreseen nowadays,
increasing the malady instead of relieving it; his whole body
gradually began to rot and fester, until the doctors declared
that he was past saving and would even die within a week.
(313f.)

The emperor's mistrust, which appears to be only one of many
kinds of mistrust, does not receive closer attention. Initially, it
seems only to motivate the sovereign, the supreme embodiment
of authority, who unites all powers of agency (though he is
nevertheless dependent on the information and expertise of
the court and of judges) to wish that Rotbart be present at the
execution. Mistrust thereby makes space for a knowledge and a
knowing subject that wishes to see with its *own eyes* in order to
evaluate the data produced by Rotbart's body: maybe excitations
and signs of affect, which, in the eighteenth century, within the
system of evidentiary proceedings, gain importance as data
worth being registered and protocolled (Weitin 2005 and 2009).

However, it is not the emperor's eyes that examine the wounds,
the marks and body signs, but the eyes of doctors. Conditioned
by an epistemology of suspicion (Vogl 1991), they look at a hand,
which by degenerating is dedicated to mediate something that
is detracted, invisible, and unknown. They look at the very part
of the body, which, in turn, no longer functions as a medium:
by writing, for example, or performing symbolic gestures, like
swearing an oath. The medical view intersects with the imperial
bird's eye view, but the authority of the interpretation of signs
and of expertise is displaced onto the field of science (Foucault
1973)—even if the knowledge produced there is shown to be rel-
ative and weak. It is depicted as being in danger because of the
time: nowadays, whenever "nowadays" might be, something completely different could be foreseen easily, and then it will become

outdated, turning into something of a kind quite unknown again. Aside from that, and in addition to the hegemony of medical expertise, the emperor, with his will to knowledge, is overtaken, outmaneuvered, and made obsolete in an entirely different manner—namely, it is the text itself that does not afford him an active role.

Disclosures

The emperor's mistrust, which is so minimally explicated at a contentual level, has a powerful effect on the progression of the story. Suddenly, the narration proceeds incredibly quickly—*one must know*, the narrator reveals, that Rotbart had an affair with the chambermaid Rosalie. Having since been spurned, Rosalie pretends to be Littegarde and spends the night of the crime with Rotbart and gives him the ring, which she had stolen from Littegarde. Nine months later, as the story goes, "the consequences of her immoral life became visible" (317). Rosalie names Rotbart as the father of the child and proves it with a ring that he (after all, he thought she was Littegarde) had sent to her in return for her gift to him. Supported by this "obvious piece of evidence," a petition for paternal support is submitted to the court. The court sends the testimony of Rosalie as well as the ring to the imperial tribunal in hopes of clearing up "the terrible mystery, which had become the chief topic of conversation" (317).

Rotbart, after reading the letter and being given the ring, now confesses immediately to responsibility for the Duke of Breysach's death and to having engaged the archer: "I am the murderer of my brother." With this declaration, he sinks back onto the litter and whispers his "black soul into the air." It is the body of the fratricide, instead of the innocent, that is consumed in red flames on the pyre. The moral legitimation of the duke's illegitimate son as his successor follows its juridical legitimation (Schneider 2003). Littegarde is returned to her paternal inheritance by an imperial decree and only three weeks later she celebrates her marriage to Trota.

The story finally gets—and this, actually, is surprising in a Kleist story—its happy ending: Rotbart's confession resolves the criminal case, while the sum and the concluding interpretation of the data produce a comprehensive picture of his offense and of Littegarde's innocence. The internal voice of her confidant, Trota, seems to have spoken the truth and been the key to the solution. It is, however, the emperor's mistrust that made this happy ending possible, and which ensured that the process of finding the truth could be brought so effortlessly to a conclusion. The unexpected turn of events is indebted to a mistrust that lets the story stagnate at a crucial point, which interrupts the chain of events and provides for a deferment. In other words, without the emperor's mistrust the case would have seen an entirely different conclusion—an entirely different truth: Trota and Littegarde would have long since been executed.

Amendment

It is mistrust, which, through its insistence on semantic open-ness, initiates the amendment of every decision made as a consequence of interpretation, such that data lose their pre-vious evidentiary power and consolidated knowledge begins to degenerate. Conversely, facts that initially seemed insignificant become meaningful details and new pieces of evidence, which serve to expand the body of evidence: because it begins to fester, Rotbart's apparently insignificant wound becomes a meaningful trace that leads to the black soul of the terrible. At the same time, it is only the delay in the execution of the sentence that can con-firm Rotbart's belief that he himself was deceived.

Eyewitness accounts from tower guards and a lady's maid, about which the text has said little or nothing up until this point, can now be brought into play. Newly introduced data receive consideration: the first ring, initially and falsely used as an alibi for Rotbart, and as evidence of Littegarde's moral failing, now testifies to the moral failing of her thieving chambermaid and is chained to a second ring, which testifies to both the paternity of a child conceived out of wedlock and the deceptive bait and switch carried out by the maid. A suit for paternal support can be tied to the remarkable legal proceedings, and because they are united in this manner, can collaborate on the decipherment of the terrible mystery. All at once, the relevant connections providing agency are easy to recognize (Geuss 2015, 106).

Mistrust functions here to set the narration in motion and to efficiently direct it to its "good" ending—not, then, the emperor himself. And Trota's discursively incommunicable faith does just as little to effect the turn in events. Even if it seems as though he always knew, his feeling must first turn into an overwhelming evidentiary burden and be certified by a confession. That these clear data have any effect at all can be ascribed only to the decel-erating delays of mistrust.

Polyvalence, Uncertainty, and Dubiousness of Data

This mistrust, which interrupts in order to effect the rapid acceleration in the deciphering of enigmatic events at the level of narration and brings them to their end in no more than *two* paragraphs, replaces an uneconomic and notoriously unprofit-able narrative mode—a mistrusting narrative mode, which attaches a provision to all information. The emperor's mistrust is tied to a mistrust that the text produces relentlessly. Up until this penultimate paragraph, in which the text finally discloses that which had been held in reserve through an interruption in the narrated action—the very thing that *one must know* in order to resolve the case—the text systematically multiplies the pos-sible interpretations and connections until they are endless; it obscures and veils itself like the clever chambermaid. The text dictates the borders of knowledge—and presents itself as a netting of clear and indistinct explanations, of "plain speech and insinuation" (294).

What it doesn't narrate is that which one might *want to know*: why the court doesn't once take into account the fact that Rotbart could have hired someone to carry out the deed intended to secure the throne for him, and why his motive is never considered. Or even why the widow of the Duke, whose very first inquiries demonstrate that the murder weapon, namely the arrow, came from Rotbart's armory, an inquiry that also reveals that Rotbart was not in his castle at the time of the murder, then expresses her displeasure that the "ambiguous disclosures" of these researched charges (which she reads "twice through attentively") should have been publically raised given that it was such an "uncertain and delicate matter," and fears "any ill-considered action" (290). All of this despite the fact that the Duke had said on his deathbed, with broken words which she "then scarcely understood," that he suspected his brother of the crime (320)—a statement the widow doesn't remember until it assembles with the body of evidence, Rotbart's confession and death grinding out the truth.

Also inexplicable is why Littegarde refers to Trota. And why she, in turn, appears to him to be worthy of his trust. In being called to defend her honor, what sustains this faith in her innocence and makes him so decisively swear to prove that innocence, not in court but in a public event—the life and death ordeal of divine combat? All that, and much, much more remains shady.

Any possible contextual meaning, on the other hand, is constantly compromised. In the text, the polyvalence, uncertainty, and dubiousness of data, of signs, events, witnesses, statements, and facts—through which the truth is supposed to appear—is directly thematized. The chamberlain engages in two verbal duels that *directly* precede the emperor's mistrust, first with his mother and then with Littegarde (Schuller 2000, 200), and says he can ignore divine judgment, forcing a climax of confusion and enigma as well as of epistemic crisis. Friedrich calls the temporal boundaries of divine combat into question, most especially its endpoint, at which God has delivered his judgment, and simultaneously assesses its conclusion as a construable statement (Reuß 1994, 19).

For the mother, the meaning of this divine statement does not remain dark, as she appeals to the authority of the law, according to which "a duel which has been declared by the judges to be concluded cannot be resumed." For Friedrich, however, the duel was brought to an end because of a "trifling accident" (307f.). "Arbitrary human laws" do not concern him. And in a certain sense rightly so: only because none of the spectators had doubted, as it is said, his death, the emperor, who is responsible for nothing more than compliance with the rules (Foucault 2002, 713), brought the fight to an end. As can be seen through the healing of the chamberlain's wounds, which weren't fatal after all, this decision was arbitrary and coincidental. For this reason alone, divine judgment becomes complex and multivalent.

What One Can Know

The text thereby fundamentally problematizes the difficulty, even the impossibility, of determining the limits and defining the truth about an event. Exactly that which *one must know* and therefore also that which one *can* know, is known in *The Duel* by exactly one agent: the invisible and omnipotent narrator. He—and not the emperor—figures as an ideal eyewitness, who advocates the truth of the occurrences and verifies them (Vogl 1991), but, at the same time, organizes, filters, and distributes data. He by himself is the authoritarian principle who organizes the forms of data deemed relevant, and of those to be removed, discarded, or declared trivial.

He is the sovereign and the data processor who assesses and rates. Similar to a search algorithm like PageRank, which arranges what one will possibly know by assigning data to positions on the hit list, his guiding criteria are unsearchable and inscrutable—they remain (despite being an aesthetic and not a Google company) secret (Bergermann 2013, 100f.). But in contradistinction to the digital gatekeepers of the unending space of the Internet, he makes explicit the act of selection, of focusing on one thing, which is therefore invariably a choice to ignore another

(Proctor 2008, 7), the act of ranking, of indexing and indication.
By twice revealing that which *one must know*, at least in these two
short moments, he identifies and draws attention as well as suspicion to himself and his manipulative procedures.

The narrator exposes himself as the one who monopolizes the
flow of information as a manipulation tactic. And he arranges the
possible clues so wastefully and wildly that the emperor, as it is
said, goes crazy as a result.[3] His politics is one of concealing transparency, which Geuss describes in reference to digital cultures
as often just as effective as the suppression and withholding of
facts for procuring absolute secrecy. It is a politics that introduces
so much that is irrelevant and misleading into the churning
stream of information that both the contentual relation and the
foundations through which determinations of knowledge and
non-knowledge are made can no longer be recognized (Geuss
2015, 106f.). Hence, finally, he is the one who communicates
without anybody ever being on a par with him.

Taking Side with Non-Knowledge

Kleist's *The Duel* makes the nameless emperor's mistrust become
the mistrust felt by the nameless reader, who must wait until
that which *one must know* reaches him coincidentally. The novella
does not do this, however, without transposing a clear and direct
speech, through which the truth can appear, into the conditional.
The final act of the emperor in the narration is namely this:

> he gave orders that in the statutes governing the sacred
> ordeal by combat, at all points where they assume that such
> a trial immediately brings guilt to light, the words "if it be
> God's will" were to be inserted. (320)

3   The English translation describes his condition much more lightly:
     "somewhat shaken in his belief" (302).

The text closes with a correction that means as much as carrying the institution of divine combat itself *ad absurdum* (Reuß 1994, 7). The medium of assumed immediate enlightenment loses its vigor. Even God's dictum becomes devaluated, being now only decisive conditionally and under certain circumstances. Even God as the singular agent, who is lord over all of the data, who knows the present in all of its details, who can therefore meticulously describe and know the past and future of all worldly events—just as the probability theoretician Laplace conceptualized the conditional intelligence later known as the Demon in 1814 (Laplace 1932, 1f.), and as the protagonist Mae Holland, on entering the campus of *The Circle* for the first time thinks, "MY GOD … It's heaven" (Eggers 2013, 1)—this agent appears in Kleist as incalculable and unreliable. Every data point, every event, every little piece of information is thereby provided with a degree of im/possibility and placed in a gray area between knowledge and non-knowledge (Schäffner 1999, 123)—where it remains.

The last act of this mistrustful, nameless emperor, therefore, dispenses entirely with the idea of making data transparent, citing the systematic impossibleness and narrowness of transparency itself. And this act runs contrary to the efforts that were current in 1800, and also runs contrary to the digitalized phantasm of the knowledge society of today. In contradistinction to those anti-political apologists of the Internet whose mistrust is directed toward institutions and critical faculties with their expertise— because they are so sure they are able to take the sovereign's, the emperor's place, and to have at their disposal the capacities and the media needed to know everything, but who also, in the same breath, attempt to delegate the curation of big data to equally obscure agents, economic interests, or the law of the algorithms, which become more and more complex by reprogramming themselves—the text of Kleist makes an issue of the operation per se. It foments mistrust as an epistemological principle, which, at facing an abundance of data, offensively takes sides with non-knowledge. It rejects the idea of pervasion, of omniscience and omnipotence, and it would rather not know than acknowledge the status quo.

Therefore, it mobilizes contradictory imaginaries against one-and-only options, as well as against assumed perspicuities, which in respect to the algorithms governing digital cultures are the average, the standard, and the habitual. In contradistinction to an "obvious" relevance generated by PageRank, based on the citation index, for example, which counts on popularity, repetition, and frequency to guide decisions (Bergermann 2013, 101; Stalder 2015), mistrust asks persistently if everything is really as it seems—or if everything is different after all? It animates us into observing, questioning, thinking, and imagining again. The emperor's mistrust gathers the uncertainty of the scattered data from their latency.

In distinction to trust, it neither substitutes the ignorance, nor effaces the ambivalence of the data, their complexity, agility, and ephemerality—rather it insists on them and keeps them virulent. Even if the text provides an abundance of data, the emperor's mistrust reminds us that the gaps of non-knowledge are not to be eliminated: the significance, as well as the truth, only show up as random and temporary configurations. Both ignorance and knowledge are made and unmade incessantly. The text simultaneously demonstrates that communication, decision-making, political judgment, and agency need not be tied to claims of absolute truth. Maybe it's exactly the opposite: mistrust could then be a commendable posture of unsettled critique in the face of an epoch of alleged truth, of confessions, and of revelation—of total transparency directed both inwardly and outwardly.

My thanks go to Peter Kuras for his translating assistance, and to Marianne Schuller for once giving me The Duel *as a gift.*

References

Bergengruen, Maximilian. 2011. "Betrügliche Schlüsse, natürliche Regeln: Zur Beweiskraft von forensischen und literarischen Indizien in Kleists *Der Zweikampf.*" In *Ausnahmezustand der Literatur: Neue Lektüren zu Heinrich von Kleist*, edited by Nicolas Pethes, 133–165. Göttingen: Wallstein.

Bergermann, Ulrike. 2013. "Linkspeicher Google: Zum Verhältnis von PageRank und Archäologie des Wissens." In idem. *Verspannungen: Vermischte Texte*, 95–116. Münster/Hamburg/Berlin/London: Lit.

Beyes, Timon, and Claus Pias. 2018. "Secrecy, Transparency, and Non-Knowledge." In *Non-Knowledge and Digital Cultures*, edited by Andreas Bernard, Matthias Koch, and Martina Leeker, 39–51, Lüneburg: meson press.

Bies, Michael, and Michael Gamper, eds. 2012. *Literatur und Nicht-Wissen. Historische Konstellationen 1730–1930*. Zürich/Berlin: diaphanes.

Eggers, Dave. 2013. *The Circle*. New York/Toronto: Knopf.

Fleig, Anne. 2013. "Unbedingtes Vertrauen: Kleists Erzählung *Der Zweikampf.*" In *Risiko – Experiment – Selbstentwurf: Kleists radikale Poetik*, edited by Hans Richard Brittnacher and Irmela von der Lühe, 96–109. Göttingen: Wallstein.

Foucault, Michel. 1973. *The Birth of the Clinic: An Archaeology of Medical Perception*. New York: Pantheon.

Foucault, Michel. 2002. "Die Wahrheit und die juristischen Formen." In idem. *Dits et Ecrits II*, edited by Daniel Defert and François Ewald, 669–792. Frankfurt am Main: Suhrkamp.

Frevert, Ute, ed. 2003. *Vertrauen: Historische Annäherungen*. Göttingen: Vanderhoeck & Ruprecht.

Frevert, Ute. 2013. *Vertrauensfragen: Eine Obsession der Moderne*. München: Beck.

Geuss, Raymond. 2015. "Republik, Markt, Demokratie." In Jacques de Saint Victor. *Die Antipolitischen*, 97–110 (commentary on *Die Antipolitischen*). Hamburg: Hamburger Edition.

Hahn, Torsten. 2008. *Das schwarze Unternehmen: Zur Funktion der Verschwörung bei Friedrich Schiller und Heinrich von Kleist*. Heidelberg: Winter.

Han, Byung-Chul. 2013. *Transparenzgesellschaft*. Berlin: Matthes & Seitz.

Hardin, Russell. 2004. *Trust and Trustworthiness*. New York: Russel Sage Foundation.

Hardin, Russell. 2006. *Trust*. Malden: Polity Press.

Hartmann, Martin. 2011. *Die Praxis des Vertrauens*. Frankfurt am Main: Suhrkamp.

Hendriks, Frank. 2014. "Democracy in The Circle: A Route to Reconnection and Engagement?" *INLOGOV Blog*. Accessed April 16, 2016. https://inlogov. com/2014/06/13/democracy-in-the-circle.

Kleist, Heinrich von. 1994. *Der Zweikampf: Brandenburger Ausgabe*. Basel/Frankfurt am Main: Stroemfeld.

Kleist, Heinrich von. 1978. "The Duel." In *The Marquise of O. and Other Stories*, translated by David Luke and Nigel Reeves. Harmondsworth/New York: Penguin.

Laplace, Pierre-Simon de. 1932. *Philosophischer Versuch über die Wahrscheinlichkeit*. Leipzig: Akademische Verlagsgesellschaft.

Luhmann, Niklas. 2009. *Vertrauen: Ein Mechanismus der Reduktion sozialer Komplexität*. Stuttgart: Lucius & Lucius.

Proctor, Robert. 2008. "Agnotology: A Missing Term to Describe the Cultural Production of Ignorance (and Its Study)." In *Agnotology: The Making and Unmaking of Ignorance*, edited by Robert Proctor and Londa Schiebinger, 1–33. Stanford: Stanford University Press.

Reemtsma, Jan Philipp. 2008. *Vertrauen und Gewalt: Versuch über eine besondere Konstellation der Moderne*. Hamburg: Hamburger Edition.

Reuß, Roland. 1994. "Mit gebrochenen Worten: Zu Kleists Erzählung *Der Zweikampf*." In *Brandenburger Kleist-Blätter* 7, 3–41. Basel/Frankfurt am Main: Stroemfeld.

Saint Victor, Jacques de. 2015. *Die Antipolitischen*. Hamburg: Hamburger Edition.

Schäffner, Wolfgang. 1999. "Nicht-Wissen um 1800: Buchführung und Statistik." In *Poetologien des Wissens um 1800*, edited by Joseph Vogl, 123–144. München: Fink.

Schneider, Helmut. 2003. "Der Sohn als Erzeuger: Zum Zusammenhang politischer Genealogie und ästhetischer Kreativität bei Heinrich von Kleist." In *Kleist-Jahrbuch 2003*, 46–62. Stuttgart: Metzler-Verlag.

Schneider, Manfred. 2013. *Transparenztraum. Literatur, Politik, Medien und das Unmögliche*. Berlin: Matthes & Seitz.

Schuller, Marianne. 2000. "Pfeil und Asche: Zu *Kleists* Erzählung Der *Zweikampf*." In *Kleist-Jahrbuch 1999*, 194–203. Stuttgart: Metzler-Verlag.

Stalder, Felix. 2015. *Die Politik der Digitalität: Zwischen Postdemokratie und Commons*. Lecture at the Digital Cultures Research Lab. Accessed April 16, 2016. https://vimeo.com/121378308.

Starobinski, Jean. 1988. *Rousseau: Eine Welt von Widerständen*. München: Hanser.

Vogl, Joseph. 1991. "Mimesis und Verdacht: Skizze zu einer Poetologie des Wissens nach Foucault." In *Spiele der Wahrheit: Foucaults Denken*, edited by François Ewald and Bernhard Waldenfels, 193–204. Frankfurt am Main: Suhrkamp.

Vogl, Joseph. 2010. "Zur Pathologie der Netzwerke." Accessed April 16, 2016. https://www.youtube.com/watch?v=2p7obIDfwoc.

Weitin, Thomas. 2005. "Melancholie und Medienwahn. Bedingungen authentischen Lesens und Schreibens bei Goethe, Lavater und Haller." In *Wahn – Wissen – Institution: Undisziplinierbare Näherungen*, edited by Karl-Josef Pazzini, Marianne Schuller, and Michael Wimmer, 117–136. Bielefeld: Transcript.

Weitin, Thomas. 2009. "Der Auftritt des Zeugen: Zeichenprozesse zwischen Literatur und Recht." *Deutsche Vierteljahrsschrift* 83: 179–190.

NON-KNOWLEDGE

UNKNOWLEDGE

KNOWLEDGE

ONTOLOGY

DIGITALITY

ABSTRACTION

OBJECTS

Digitality, (Un)knowledge, and the Ontological Character of Non-Knowledge

Alexandre Monnin

The dialectic between knowledge and non-knowledge may obscure the very fact that digitization has also "remedied" knowledge, lending it the character of a commodity instead of a norm (which it was previously considered, despite the disagreement on its proper characterization entertained by philosophers and epistemologists). Hence, one is required to situate not only non-knowledge vis-à-vis knowledge but also knowledge vis-à-vis digitization and a third term I would call "unknowledge." Non-knowledge is taken to be a necessary condition of many phenomena that are not reducible to knowledge, which, at the same time, is threatened by the generalization of digitally fueled unknowledge.

Although we have no word for it, establishing
an appropriate degree of "middle connectivity"
to the world is such a basic feature of the
human condition that doing it successfully has
been lifted into the rarefied reaches of saint-
hood and enlightenment; failing to accomplish
it, identified as a cause of paralytic anxiety
– Brian Cantwell Smith

The relationship between knowledge, non-knowledge, and digitality is a complex one, still waiting to be fully explored. As evidenced in this volume, efforts to shed some light on "non-knowledge" open up new directions of research that are especially relevant, as we'll see, in a world becoming more digitized every day. On the other hand, as such, the opposition between knowledge and non-knowledge tends to obscure the very fact that digitization has also "remedied" knowledge, lending it the character of a commodity instead of a norm (which it was previously considered, despite the disagreement entertained by philosophers and epistemologists among themselves). Hence, one is required not only to situate non-knowledge vis-à-vis knowledge but also knowledge vis-à-vis digitization.

Knowledge, Digitality, and Unknowledge

Knowledge and Digitality: Epistemic Issues

Knowledge both admits of a vast number of characterizations and comes in different flavors. While it is possible to hold shared views on the purview of knowledge while at the same time disagreeing on its exact definition, disagreement may still loom over the horizon. Whether tacit or practical knowledge refers to a phenomenon that can be subsumed under one heading along with scientific knowledge, or knowledge as traditionally conceived

by epistemologists, is a question that remains largely open to
debate.

For that reason, it would at first glance seem illusory to contrast
(and not necessarily to oppose) a unified concept of knowledge
with non-knowledge. Yet, without such a unified concept,
the need for a correlative unified concept of non-knowledge
becomes, at best, moot. The best-known philosophical answer
to the question, "What exactly is knowledge?" has long been
"justified true belief." Despite the paradoxes this definition
lends itself to (in particular the Gettier problem), let us take it
as a departure point and add that knowledge is knowledge of a
referent, whether in the form of an accurate description of it or
true predictions regarding its behavior, etc.

What about digitization, then? Digitization and knowledge have
a complex and quite paradoxical relationship. Going back to
the concept of "knowledge economy,"[1] made possible by the
advances of digitization, one immediately sees this relation for
what it is: a relation of commodification. "Knowledge" in the
knowledge economy no longer denotes any norm or domain
(which it merely connotes) but rather betokens a broad assim-
ilation to a commodity, essentially cultivated in order to sustain
growth. Both the normative and pluralistic aspects of knowledge
have as a consequence seemingly vanished or at least been
largely obscured.

While paradoxical, this evolution shouldn't come as a surprise for
it may very well characterize digitization as such. As a result, one
of the claims in this paper will be that digitality has both overplayed *and* downplayed salient aspects of knowledge, to the point
that we might, on initial approximation, think of this evolution as
bringing knowledge nearer to its negation, what might be called
"non-knowledge." As we shall see, however, as we progressively
move away from epistemic questions, the case for introducing an

1   See Christoph Wulf's contribution to this volume.

additional category and situating non-knowledge on a different plane will become more and more compelling.

Overplayed, I would argue, because conceptual knowledge already grasps its referent in a simplified way, if only to articulate true propositions where, for instance, proper nouns denote individuals, and common nouns denote properties (a conceit still used within logical artificial intelligence (AI)). Mathematical models, despite potentially being very complex, must nonetheless simplify reality in order to allow for more accurate predictions. In this regard, they may be revised to accommodate some of the minute details of a world they never exhaust. Science, then, produces knowledge about the world but not necessarily one conclusive picture.

Now, with digitality, models and abstractions have become not only a sign of the portability of conceptual knowledge but also a means to perform assemblages that *induce* new realities instead of deferring, one way or another, to some preexisting world— again in the name of simplification and formalization. Make no mistake: deferring to the world involves taking into account the intricate ways in which the world is being transformed by our own activity—especially in the Anthropocene! That said, digitization tends to consider its models within its own reality without always properly deferring to the world. Google's PageRank algorithm is a good example. It construes incoming hyperlinks as votes or endorsements (never as signs of defiance!) in its willingness to redefine the web by using measures of authority, while *pretending* to remain neutral—even though its own existence modifies the very topology of the thing it was supposed to measure independently.

And then *downplayed* since the commodification of knowledge, made possible by the lack of regard for traditional norms of knowledge (in a sense "anything goes" in the knowledge economy so long as its goals are achieved), resulted in more and more data, metadata, documents, and so on and so forth—what I would term "knowledge traces"—being produced, gathered and made available with unforeseen consequences that are well worth examining.

Innovation is better served, or so it seems, by people who have little regard for the minutiae of everyday life, assured as they are of the well-foundedness of their mission to transform it. Of course, one may ask a) How and why on earth should that which is not well enough grasped be transformed? And b) Is it even possible to ensure that the replacement (or modification) is something genuinely *new*? One could argue regarding the second objection that only induction through enumeration would provide a proper answer, and it is well known to be insufficient. Let's put it aside then because, basically, we have to live with similar "uncertainties."

The answer to the first objection is much less straightforward. Digital technologies produce *new assemblages* while at the same time claiming to operationalize *preexisting realities* (intelligence, authority, vote, trust, etc.). Changing the meaning of those concepts/values/realities is seldom, if ever, an explicit goal. Rather, these realities are generally taken for granted and whether the ensuing operationalization turns out to be something wholly different, even in logical contradiction to what they previously stood for, is no one's business.

Assemblages and performance have always marched hand in hand since assemblages perform, by definition, a specific effect. (Centre de Sociologie de l'Innovation 2013). And from that arises the legitimate fear that focusing on assemblages alone might obfuscate any reference (and deference) to the world. Yet, the lack of regard displayed by innovators concerns not just the world but also the assemblages produced therein (the subsequent operationalization is always made with reference to preexisting realities, resulting in a common neglecting of both sides of the equation: that which is being operationalized and the end result of such operationalizations).

Thus, we go from knowledge to what we'd call "unknowledge"—introducing this concept in order to characterize a specific contrast to knowledge akin to a lack of willingness to defer/refer to the world that is still unabashedly regarded as fully fledged knowledge.

Unknowledge is very well illustrated by this quote from Phil Agre about AI:

> As a practical matter, the purpose of AI is to build computer systems whose operation can be narrated using intentional vocabulary. Innovations frequently involve techniques that bring new vocabulary into the field: reasoning, planning, learning, choosing, strategizing, and so on. Whether the resulting systems are really exhibiting these qualities is hard to say, and AI people generally treat the question as an *annoying irrelevance* [my emphasis]. What matters practically is not the vague issue of what the words "really mean" but the seemingly precise issue of how they can be defined in formal terms that permit suitably narratable systems to be designed. If you disapprove of the way that we formalize the concept of reasoning or planning or learning, they are likely to say, then you are welcome to invent another way to formalize it. (Agre 1997)[2]

Unknowledge prolongs knowledge insofar as it seemingly shares the aim of formalizing phenomena, thus leaving aside part of their richness. Yet, unlike knowledge, always revisable and never able to exhaust what there is, unknowledge, by materializing and making directly operational its representations, is in danger of losing sight of its referent and becoming self-referential (digital formalizations are also a lot more expensive than pen and paper ones!). This is what Agre means with the quote above: in the end,

2   I have suggested (Monnin 2015) that the roots of formalization thus conceived lie in Rudolf Carnap's concept of "explication," to which scholars have turned their attention in recent years; see especially Carus 2007 and Richardson 2013.

what the "words 'really mean'" or what the world really is matters
less than the design of new workable formal systems. We can
thus conceive of unknowledge as a contemporary pathology
of knowledge, albeit one that is rooted in some core aspects
of knowledge itself, namely abstraction and/or discretization
(without distinguishing them yet)—two essential forms of simplification that are nevertheless always in need of a careful
reining in.

Non-Knowledge and Unknowledge:
An Ontological Characterization

With unknowledge in sight, what can be said about non-
knowledge? Brian Cantwell Smith contends that *content*, a
technical term used in analytic philosophy to designate the basis
of knowledge and action, can be either *conceptual* or *non-conceptual*. *Conceptual content* involves positing a world consisting
of objects, properties and relations, which amounts to carving
reality into discretized individuals (seen as the bearers of
properties and in relation to one another). *Non-conceptual content*, while still representational, registers the world not in the
same way but rather in terms of un-individuated "features" that
precede the advent of objects or individuals—something which,
for Smith, is essentially an ethical matter (a matter of "mattering"
as he puts it). The picture offered by non-conceptual content is
essentially a "subobjective"[3] one. Whereas non-conceptual content depicts the world in overwhelming detail, fit for situated and
local encounters, conceptual content and objectivity in general
strip it of those same details so as to make it possible to make
reference over long distances (to distant things, things long gone

---

3   See Lowe 1992, whose subtitle is composed of three texts by Adrian Cussin,
     Brian Cantwell Smith and Bruno Latour (currently being translated by the
     author).

and buried in the past, not yet born in a distant future, or too shrouded in vagueness to do otherwise).[4]

With objects and ontology predicated on ethics (in Smith's sense), what remains metaphysically indispensable is to give room to reference-making. That is, to articulate causally effective local encounters with the world with non-causal long-distance reference. In other words, what is valued here is less one over-arching metaphysical category (the One, the transcendental a priori, Ideas, the Body and so on) than the room needed to conceive of both proximal connections and distal reference:

> [I]t is essential ... and also an anchor of common sense, that the multi-various parts of the world do not march in lockstep together. The world is fundamentally character-ized by an underlying flex or slop—a kind of slack or "play" that allows some bits to move about or adjust without much influencing, and without being much influenced by, other bits. ... As a contrast, therefore, imagine a world quite unlike ours, consisting, ... of nothing but an endless series of inter-locked gears. Suppose ... that every gear is constructed so as to mesh with one or more immediate neighbors, and that the entire gear universe is interconnected, but in such a way that it is still possible for them all to be turned ... so that it does not lock up. Suppose, too, that the gears are perfect: no friction, no play between the teeth .... The gear world would lack slop. Effects would not dissipate. If one gear were to move by even a tiny amount, every other gear

4   "Perhaps the best way to summarize this is by an analogy. I sometimes think of objects, properties, and relations (i.e., conceptual, material ontology) as the long-distance trucks and interstate highway systems of intentional, normative life. They are undeniably essential to the overall integration of life's practices—critical, given finite resources, for us to integrate the vast and open-ended terrain of experience into a single, cohesive, objective world. But the cost of packaging up objects for portability and long-distance travel is that they are thereby insulated from the extraordinarily fine-grained richness of particular, indigenous life—insulated from the ineffable richness of the very lives they sustain." (Cantwell Smith, draft, 37).

in the universe, no matter how far flung, would instantly and proportionally be affected. … If the flex were too little … the world would lock up like the gear world, and everything would be correlated with everything else. Such a world would be too rigid, too straight, too stuffy; intentionality would be neither possible nor necessary. If the flex were too great, on the other hand, it would have the opposite problem: things would be too loose, everything would be random, and effect-transcending coordination would be impossible. Imagine … an infinite space randomly occupied by an indefinitely large number of particles, all of which drift aimlessly around, none of which ever interact. (Cantwell Smith 1998, 199–207)[5]

Following Smith, we understand non-knowledge as the very possibility of a separation from a referent (a possibility that itself allows room to be made for "some thing," for the ontological realm of discretized objects). The paradox is then the following:[6] while non-knowledge makes it possible to refer without any

---

5   Compare with William James, who put great emphasis on the fact that "[n]ot all the parts of the world are united mechanically, for some can move without the others moving." (*Some problems of philosophy* in James 1996, 1046). Latour's project in *An Inquiry into the Modes of Existence* (Latour 2012) has been summarized the following way: "What is at stake: to take seriously the first proposition, to civilize the moderns until they do not successfully 'make room' [for] others. The inquiry indicates that the function of its metaphysics is simply to make a place," commentary signed by the GECo *(Groupe d'Etudes Constructivistes)* on the online version of Latour 2012. Available at: http://modesofexistence.org/inquiry/#a=-SET+DOC+LEADER&c[leading]=DOC&c[slave]=TEXT&i[id]=#doc-257&-i[column]=DOC&s=0&q=make+room, accessed February 26, 2017. Giving room to modes of existence (whether modern or non-modern) is the new diplomatic goal of "metaphysics." Of peculiar interest here is the fact that modes of existence themselves are all described by certain kinds of continuity and discontinuity ("hiatuses"). This is very much in tune with Smith. So much so, in fact, that it generalizes it in a pluralistic fashion. While a systematic comparative study of Smith's and Latour's positions hasn't been undertaken, it would definitely be a task well worth embarking on.

6   I would like to express thanks to Pierre Livet who read an earlier version of this paper and pointed out this paradox.

114 causal links, unknowledge replaces reference and the referent with causal links between actionable traces—despite the fact that the relation between such traces and any referent has become an "annoying irrelevance."

At first glance, unknowledge appears to threaten long-distance reference since according to the definition we have adopted it no longer defers to the world, preoccupied as it is with its own self-centered efficiency. But such a criticism would be mistaken if left at that. While unknowledge denotes a peculiar lack of awareness of its limits, it is also defined by what it produces, namely, "knowledge traces." In other words, it adds gears where there were none, where space used to provide enough room for the "world's flex and slop," filling in preexisting gaps, favoring the multiplication of interlocked gears and short-distance com-munication to simulate continuity over long-distance reference. The strategy adopted is instead one of generalized padding, where gears can be endlessly introduced and correlated with one another. Therefore, unknowledge also raises ontological questions—rather than purely epistemic ones—by threatening the middle ground between absence and presence, distance and proximity, with its overflowing stuffiness.

The threat posed by abstraction was discussed at the beginning of this paper. At this point, the picture becomes more complex. Indeed, one must make an additional distinction to properly account for the risks induced by unknowledge. Conceptual formalization is one form of abstraction. On the other hand, digital formalization partakes in abstraction while at the same time being very much concrete: actual and not just virtual in the strict philosophical sense of these words. So much so that in the end unknowledge materializes formal abstractions (which, accordingly, are no longer abstractions, strictly speaking). The ensuing risk is twofold: a) by adding a layer of connected formal traces either "on top" of distal referents or which "stand for" those, we may no longer be concerned with what we are not locally and causally connected to (which, incidentally, represents

most of the world!) and that we can only apprehend through separation and distal reference—we need to be able to partially dis-
connect ourselves from our local surroundings to get a broader
grasp of the world; and b) by neglecting the fact that what is
digitized or materialized is nothing but the representation of an
abstraction (a referent) that it may never completely exhaust, we
tend to forget that such formal representations may very well
misrepresent their referents—as they inevitably do.[7]

Love and Felicity and Subsistence

I will address the way these ontological issues manifest
themselves concretely by looking at the example of love, as
studied by Eva Illouz in her inquiry on how new digital life shapes
our most intimate relationships.[8] Illouz identifies that romantic
encounters become increasingly saturated by knowledge
practices. Thanks to the generalization of online profiles and the
metadata they contain, knowledge's role has gone awry, oblit-
erating, as she puts it, other types of relations and reshuffling the
boundaries between proximity and distance (an ontological feat
of no little consequence, as we have seen).

Nowhere else is the subtle dialectic between absence and
presence, distance and proximity, more at play than in the
phenomenon called "love." It is not surprising then that
unbalancing this relation with knowledge (under the guise of
unknowledge) should put it at risk. Before intimacy grew to
become a norm, we had never known that much about our love
interests. Additionally, before the advent of digital cultures, social

---

7   P. Livet understands what Smith treats as abstractions as a virtual element
    of a specific ontological kind. I am with him there but cannot discuss this
    point much further.

8   Her presentation at the Centre for Digital Cultures (CDC) during the winter
    semester, dedicated to non-knowledge and entitled "Knowing way too
    much... Love, Therapy, Technology," is available online: https://vimeo.
    com/153692828, accessed February 28, 2017.

networks, online profiles and the like, we never knew that much about our *potential* love interests ahead of encountering them.

It could be assumed that the boundaries of personhood in a relationship have by and large been displaced. While profiles do seem to provide accurate (if coarse) knowledge, making visible "who" we are by maintaining the boundaries of our identity, what in fact happens is that they delegate (outsource, really) what was previously left to chance encounters to algorithms that calculate our best match.

Of course, pretending that love owes nothing to chance is not entirely new either. Sociology, for one, is a discipline that literally saw its mission (as opposed to novel writing for instance) as the shedding of light onto the social dynamics underneath the most intimate and private phenomena, including lovers' attraction. It held dear and strived to uncover the unseen determinants at play behind the curtain. And it was correct in its own right, of course. There's no denying that love might not escape (at least some measure of) determinism.

We should nonetheless pay heed to a paramount difference between these two cases: while sociologists did provide statistical conclusions in favor of their claims, no one ever (mis)took them as spiritual advisers. In a sense, so much has happened with the advent of social networks and dating websites. Filling in innumerable fields on a daily basis means people become both providers *and* consumers of the (un)knowledge thus produced about themselves. Whereas sociologists' scientific take on love used to be discussed mainly among peers or an educated readership with an interest in the *discipline,* it may be said to have now infused many, if not most, of our daily transactions, and what is more, in a degraded state.

Then again, such a move might be readily welcomed. Aren't relationships, now that we can mimic the behaviors and functional possibilities of connected objects (especially the localization bit and the availability of "leaky" knowledge traces), the better for it? After all, no philosophical talk will likely dispel the belief that cheating is cheating and that cell phones (undoubtedly the Internet of Thing's first citizen) do provide an efficient way to learn the truth in this matter. Must we eventually backtrack on the criticism of unknowledge if deferring to the world means deferring to such simple truths?

The point is rather that deferring to the world might precisely mean something else, at least as far as love is concerned. Bruno Latour (2012) suggests that we adopt a pluralistic view on metaphysics so as to give space to phenomena that are amenable to specific felicitous or infelicitous conditions. Going back to Agre's remark, we may begin to understand why digitality is by no means harmless. Digital tools do promise transparency. It is all too easy then to treat love as demanding it. Paying heed to the felicitous conditions of love should, however, advise otherwise. Indeed, the latter may lie less in the search for truth (or knowledge) than in love's own subsistence; a matter of delicate, fine-spun dialectic between proximity and distance, presence and absence, knowledge and non-knowledge, put at risk when (un)knowledge takes over in its "profusing transparency" (talk of "transparency" bears witness to an interesting choice of words, as the immediate danger is either to be *blinded* by the abundance of digital traces of all kinds or to treat them indeed as transparent intermediaries). However, in order to properly understand the key role played by non-knowledge with regards to love one has to overcome unknowledge first.

Not unlike love, art also has its own conditions of felicity. Subsistence, then, may adequately translate into being able to listen to the call of the work of art (to speak Etienne Souriau's language).[9] And that might imply an obfuscation of part of the creative process if needs be. Immediately, the question arises, "does it amount to lying?" Whenever truth is equated with transparency, with little or no regard for the phenomenon at stake, the answer

9   See Souriau 2009 and 1955.

is yes. By contrast, when subsistence, understood as the continuation of the phenomenon at stake, takes priority, the answer shall be a clear "no," knowledge at that point being subservient to care. This is reminiscent of "ethnographic refusal," a decision not to write about a subject matter to avoid putting it at risk, being exploitative or unhelpful (among the many traps that await researchers in that field).[10]

Latour himself expresses the need for a "crooked language" in politics as well:

> [N]othing is more important for this inquiry than to find the difference between truth and falsity in politics. If there is one area where our inheritance has to be revisited, it is surely that of the hopes placed in politics and its capacity for extension. What will we have to do to situate appropriately crooked speaking once again at the center of our civility as the only means to collect the collective, and above all to universalize it? Does the Circle give us a thread like Ariadne's that will let us speak here again of the rational and the irrational but in a well-curved way, that is, in its own language, provided that we don't seek to judge it with the help of a different touchstone? We need this thread, for how could we stand up straight on the agora, with no hope of help from any Science and yet without giving up on reason, about controversial issues that have taken on the dimensions of the planet and in the heat of a crowd that now numbers in the billions? (Latour 2012)[11]

10   A note on ethnographic refusal with a bibliography was recently published online: https://discardstudies.com/2016/08/08/ethnographic-refusal-a-how-to-guide/, accessed February 28, 2017.

11   Online notes available at: http://modesofexistence.org/inquiry/?lang=en#b[chapter]=#29&b[subhead ing]=#541&a=-SET+TEXT+LEADER&c[leading]=TEXT&c[slave]=VOC&s=0&q=nothing+is+m ore+important+for+this+inquiry+than+to+find+the+difference, accessed February 28, 2017.

Contrary to Latour, I would not restrict such a crooked language **119** to politics. Or rather, to put it more succinctly, this kind of language can be seen as the political answer provided to a broader issue. With respect to non-knowledge, we have come to give precedence to subsistence over those truths obtained by producing oversimplifications.[12] Subsistence requires care[13] and a hospitable middle ground, whether in politics, love, or the arts. Unknowledge, by contrast, unable as it is to defer to the world even as it conveys trite truths, striving to unbalance the middle ground, sorely lacks this aspect. As Agre puts it, "a reformed technical practice [should] employ the tools of critical inquiry to engage in a richer and more animated conversation with the world" (1995). For this conversation with the world to be genuinely fruitful, non-knowledge should be neither overlooked nor undermined.

Conclusion

Crooked language is no enemy of reason, yet neither is it to be understood in terms of truth or falsity as science understands it. As we have seen, non-knowledge, unlike knowledge (and to a lesser extent unknowledge, which is not just a degraded epistemic norm but also has an ontological dimension), is less an epistemic value than a *metaphysical middle ground* allowing for

12   "Add some transparency, some truth (still in the sense of Double Click), and you still get only dissolution, stampede, the dispersal of that very agora in which the fate of all categories is judged." http://modesof-existence.org/inquiry/?lang=en#b[chapter]=#13&b[subheading]=#211&a=-SET+TEXT+LEADER&c[leading]=TEXT&c[slave]=VOC&s=0&q=agora, accessed February 26, 2017.

13   This was tacitly acknowledged in a recent tweet published on the AIME (An Inquiry into Modes of Existence) account: "It's one hypothesis of AIME that beings of [POL] are so fragile that their mode of existence may disappear entirely through lack of care." Available at: https://twitter.com/AIMEproject/status/756786152548409344, accessed February 26, 2017. That the generalization is not made outside [POL] is a testament of Latour's rather complex relationship to care.

the subsistence of a multiplicity of generic phenomena according to their own requirements (akin to Latour's modes of existence). William James himself noted that "the same thing … can belong to many systems, as when a man is connected with other objects by heat, by gravitation, by love, *and by knowledge* [my emphasis]" (1996, 1048). Tellingly, knowledge in his enumeration was but one among many such systems.

James also noticed our relentless propensity to add what he called new "systems of concatenation": "We ourselves are constantly adding to the connection of things, organizing labor unions, establishing postal consular, mercantile, railroad, telegraphs, colonial, and other systems that bind us and things together in ever wider reticulations" (ibid.). It is somewhat ironic that we only have a negative expression like "non-knowledge" at our disposal to refer to the multiplicity of these systems of concatenations minus one… Such is the overwhelming weight of unknowledge today: no longer a norm but rather a system of concatenations that not only overshadows and twists others but eventually jeopardizes their conditions of subsistence.

I would like to thank the CDC for the kind invitation to be involved in the semester dedicated to non-knowledge as a fellow in November 2015, and to express particular gratitude to Martina Leeker.

References

Agre, Philip E. 1995. "The Soul Gained and Lost." *Stanford Humanities Review* 4 (2): 1–19.

Agre, Philip E. 1997. "Toward a Critical Technical Practice: Lessons Learned in Trying to Reform AI." In *Bridging the Great Divide: Social Science, Technical Systems, and Cooperative Work*, edited by Geoffrey C. Bowker, Les Gasser, Susan Leigh Star, and William Turner. New York: Erlbaum Press.

Cantwell Smith, Brian. 1998. *On the Origin of Objects*. Cambridge, MA: MIT Press.

Cantwell Smith, Brian. "The Nonconceptual World." (unpublished draft paper)

Carus, A. W. 2007. *Carnap and Twentieth-Century Thought Explication as Enlightenment*. Cambridge: Cambridge University Press.

Centre de Sociologie de l'Innovation. 2013. *Sociologie des agencements marchands: textes choisis*. Paris: Mines ParisTech.

James, William. 1996. *Writings: 1902–1910*. Published as *The Library of America 38*, edited by Bruce Kuklick. New York: Literary Classics of the United States.

Latour, Bruno. 2012. *Enquête sur les modes d'existence: Une anthropologie des Modernes*. Paris: Éditions La Découverte.

Lowe, Adam. 1992. *Registration Marks: Metaphors for Subobjectivity*. London, UK: Pomeroy Purdy Gallery.

Monnin, Alexandre. 2015. "L'ingénierie philosophique de Rudolf Carnap: De l'IA au Web sémantique." *Cahiers philosophiques* 141 (2): 27. Accessed February 26, 2017. doi:10.3917/caph.141.0027.

Richardson, Alan. 2013. "Taking the Measure of Carnap's Philosophical Engineering: Metalogic as Metrology." In *The Historical Turn in Analytic Philosophy*, edited by Erich Reck, 60–77. Basingstoke: Palgrave Macmillan.

Souriau, Étienne. 1955. *L'Ombre de Dieu*. Paris: Presses Universitaires de France.

Souriau, Étienne. 2009. *Les différents modes d'existence, suivi de De l'œuvre à faire*. Paris: Presses Universitaires de France.

UNKNOWING

SILENT KNOWLEDGE

ICONIC TURN

PERFORMATIVE TURN

MATERIAL TURN

[7]

Unknowing and Silent Knowledge as a Challenge: Iconic, Performative, and Material Perspectives

Christoph Wulf

Unknowing plays an important role in anthropology, philosophy, and cultural studies. Here, unknowing is often not considered negative but is deemed a constitutive condition of knowledge. In historical anthropology, we have picked up on this insight and understanding and, following Helmuth Plessner, assume that the human being must be understood as "homo absconditus," which itself is never completely recognizable. Following the "linguistic turn" in the final quarter of the twentieth century, there have been several "turns" in the cultural sciences (humanities), in which dealing with the limits of knowledge and tacit knowledge play an important role.

Unknowing as a Condition of the Humanities

Unknowing plays an important role in anthropology, philosophy, and cultural studies. Here, unknowing is often not considered negative but is deemed a constitutive condition of knowledge. At the end of his life, Socrates said that he knew virtually nothing. He was, however, aware of this and that the highest form of knowledge lay therein. In historical anthropology, we have picked up on this insight and understanding and, following Helmuth Plessner, assume that the human being must be understood as "homo absconditus," which itself is never completely recognizable. The concept of "deus absconditus," the unfathomable God, was coined in theology to express the inscrutability of God. According to Nietzsche's God is dead declaration, the question arises as to what extent the human being has replaced God and whether it is time to clarify in the humanities that humans are themselves unfathomable, that unknowing is a constitutive condition of human life, human insight, and historical-cultural anthropology.

This is all the truer if we assume that it is not the responsibility of science to reduce complexity, but to increase complexity by acquiring new knowledge. Ultimately, with every realization, the number of new questions generated as a result grows to the extent that cognitive processes never come to an end. Therefore, in the humanities, there is talk of the contingent character of human life and knowledge. Contingency clarifies the shortcoming of ideas, which accept gradual advance and are not open to the emergent character of knowledge, limiting its foreseeability and calculability. While in the humanities today talk is often about contingency and contingent knowledge, in many parts of the natural sciences, technical sciences, and social sciences, this dimension of knowledge is actively hidden. Uninterrupted knowledge gain and success are lauded, and thus social recognition and financing for further research are received. Science is rewarded for providing assurance and upholding the prospect

of limiting uncertainty and the fundamental contingency of
knowledge.

The emphasis on the fundamental non-overcoming of unknowing
in the humanities is contrary to science's legitimizing raison
d'être: that it can recognize and diminish the unknown.
Particularly in quantitative research, and above all in its official
and political use and reception, a "gestus" (gesture, manner) is
revealed that assumes the world is recognizable as a whole and
is, as a consequence, controllable and can be improved.

In the late 1960s and early 1970s, the positivism dispute had
already raised sustained doubt about the complacent reliance
on knowledge. In critical rationalism, advanced by Karl Popper
and others, knowledge was considered scientific if it followed a
single method believed to be correct from a normative viewpoint.
Mandatory use of the correct method, irrespective of the content,
ensured the scientific character of research results. The method
guarantees, through the reproducibility of its results, validity or
truth and thus its scientific character. Thomas Kuhn (1962) raised
doubts about this view with reference to the significance of
paradigm shifts for the acquisition of new scientific knowledge.

Even more fundamental were the objections from the
representatives of the Critical Theory against the reduction of
science to methodology. They also criticized the development
of research issues and the question of how the research results
could be used on a social level, stating that it should not be part
of science. According to this view, only the formation of "mid-
range theories," which are necessary for empirical research,
should be considered theory formation. Theories that claim to
have a broader reach and explanatory power do not belong to
science according to this opinion: they are to be viewed as part
of philosophy. Quantitative empirical research, therefore, grew
strongly in subsequent years, bolstered by an alliance with politics and business.

Other approaches in scientific development, such as the critique of the Frankfurt School of capitalism and neoliberalism, are almost forgotten today. Key concepts of Critical Theory such as "enlightenment" and "emancipation," "reification" and "critique," "sociability" and "reflexivity," "theory" and "practice," have disappeared from the vocabulary of the humanities. In contrast to the efforts of the 1960s and 1970s, when it was thought much could be overcome with a critique of inadequacies, recent decades have shown that critique and reflection are indeed important prerequisites for the improvement of social conditions, but only contribute towards this improvement to a limited extent.

In discourses on post-modernity, doubt was repeatedly cast on the value of the "grand narratives" (Lyotard 1979), which also involved the Frankfurt School. Here, there was less doubt about the quality of knowledge of the quantitative sciences and their explanatory power, i.e., about the scientism of these sciences. With reference to the previously mentioned concept of contingency, doubt was raised about the systemization, reliability, and coherence of scientific knowledge in the humanities. On several occasions, Adorno (1978) drew attention to the fact that the enlightening character of scientific knowledge may turn into its opposite and that science was in danger of contributing to the reification of humans and their relationships with the world. Derrida (1972) and others also made clear, using their idea of deconstruction, the ways in which strong knowledge and recognition are linked to certain conditions. A change in those conditions leads to a change in the logic of scientific knowledge. It is obvious that dealing with unknowing in these processes is a constitutive role.

"Turns" and Knowledge

Following the "linguistic turn" in the final quarter of the twentieth century, there have been several "turns" in the cultural sciences (humanities), in which dealing with the limits of knowledge and with tacit knowledge play an important role. I am interested in key areas described as "iconic," "performative," and "material" turns.

The iconic, performative, and material turns and their associated perspectives lead to the development of new fields of research with new purposes, methods, and results. Within the framework of each perspective, areas can be identified which are excluded because of their respective focus and which, although they are closely connected to the issues being examined, are not addressed. With a focus on images, the iconic and the media in the first key area described here, the human body—its productions, performances, and movements—as well as the materiality of technology and new media, were overlooked. This is surprising as performativity also belongs to the conditions of images and the media. This changed in the second turn, in which the perspectives omitted in the first turn became the focus of attention. Although attention was now directed at the body, its movements, its productions, and performances, the implicit silent knowledge in the body was rarely a subject. Even where talk was of practical knowledge, incorporation of the knowledge was not, or only to some extent, examined. Only where performativity was addressed in connection with mimetic processes did the significance of the implicit incorporated knowledge for social activities come into view (Wulf 2013). A focus on the materiality of media, new technologies, the body, and things in the third turn was so important it sparked the question of whether its entanglement with the subjectivity of people attracted sufficient attention, and if the plurality of the subjects and the effect of this perspective on the understanding of materiality in implicit or silent knowledge was pushed aside. This meant that the focus on the different key areas led to the suppression of other aspects.

As our study "Global Youth in Digital Trajectories" (Kontopodis, Varvantakis, and Wulf 2017)—which was financed by the European Union and involved a compilation of six case studies in Germany, The Netherlands, Greece, Russia, India, and Brazil on how young people deal with the digital world—shows, these key areas also play a role in the handling of the virtual world. Considering the importance of these areas in the humanities I would like to briefly describe them and develop some thoughts on the significance silent knowledge has here (Kraus et al. 2017). But first of all, some thoughts on what I understand by this term.

Silent Knowledge

With the distinction between "Knowing How and Knowing That," Gilbert Ryle had already, in the 1940s, drawn attention to the fact that there are different forms of knowledge, of which the practical implementations described with a "knowing how" are difficult to research (Ryle 1990). With these methods, the focus is not on the acquisition of factual knowledge that can be expressed linguistically. On the contrary, "knowing how" describes a skill that enables the person to act and which is learned in mimetic processes by referring to the practices of other people. An example of this is rituals. Rituals are not statements, reasons, or explanations. They must be staged and performed. The knowledge required for rituals is a performative, practical knowledge, which differs from the knowledge needed for the description, interpretation, and analysis of rituals. "Knowing how" is thus a practical knowledge—an incorporated skill that is visible in a person's performance. In mimetic processes today smartphones and tablets merge with the body and expand its effects beyond tight physical boundaries.

A practice such as driving a car is only learned if the explanation of how to learn was understood. But constantly remembering this explanation is not necessary to execute the action. An action cannot be "skillfully" engaged in as long as this remembering is necessary. Once the learning has been incorporated, the person has the skill to practice, i.e., to drive a car. Practical skill is thus a form of knowledge that requires attention and social recognition. Types of practical knowledge are constitutive for many sciences

such as medicine, law, and education. In the words of Ryle:
"Successful practice precedes its actual theory" (Ryle 1990, 33).

Michael Polanyi, who understands knowledge as an awareness and thinking process, as a knowing in action, writes: "I regard knowing as an active comprehension of the things known, an action that requires skill. Skillful knowing and doing is performed by subordinating a set of particulars, as clues or tools, to the shaping of a skillful achievement, whether practical or theoretical" (Polanyi 1974, VII). Polanyi indicates that if a person points at a wall using their finger and asks someone to look, the person looks at the wall and not at the finger, and concludes:

> One way is to look at a thing. This is the way you look at the wall. But how is one to describe the way you see my finger pointing at the wall? You are not looking at my finger, but away from it. I should say that you do not see it as a mere object to be examined as such, but as an object having a function: the function of directing your attention away from itself and at something else. But this is not to say that my pointing finger was trying to make you disregard itself. Far from it. It wanted to be seen, but to be seen only in order to be followed and not in order to be examined. (Polanyi 1977, 313)

This is implicit knowledge that the objective of the perception reference is the wall at which the finger is pointing and not the actual finger, and therefore the focus of awareness to the movement, and then to the wall, is required. Polanyi repeatedly refers to examples that show what he means by silent knowledge; for example, a pianist who if he concentrated on the individual movements of his fingers would become paralyzed and unable to perform. Using cycling and the balancing it requires, Polanyi explains how complex the practices of knowledge are for physical skills: "We cannot learn to keep our balance on a bicycle by taking to heart that in order to compensate for a given angle of imbalance a, we must take a curve on the side of the imbalance, of which the radius (r) should be proportionate to the square of the velocity (v) over the imbalance: … Such knowledge is ineffectual, unless known tacitly" (Polanyi 1969, 144). From this consideration, it can be concluded that: "A physical understanding of the force fields of the movements cannot obviously help with dealing with the somatic-kinaesthetic interplay of forces of balance" (Huschka 2017).

What role does silent knowledge now play in the iconic, performative, and material turns and how does it appear together with the key areas described by these terms in the digital world? The question is complex, and I can only answer it with a first approximation.

Images and Picture Character of the World

Following preliminary work by Marshall McLuhan (1964), Jean Baudrillard (1981), and Paul Virilio (1996), who examined the media and picture character of new media and emphasized their speed, ubiquity, and simulation character, several studies have emerged since the 1990s about the theory of the image and imagination. These extensive studies clarified that the increase in images as a result of media is leading to profound changes in society and culture. In addition, there were several studies that presented, in detail, the importance of the computer and the internet for the development of new forms of communication and aesthetics in the globalized world.

According to Martin Heidegger and others, the growing importance of images results from the fact that human beings have "extracted" themselves from nature or God's creations and now see the world as an object; the world has become an image (Wulf 2014). During this development, the extent to which images represent iconic knowledge that can be only inadequately recognized using language became clear. In Gotthold Ephraim Lessing's interpretation of the statue of Laocoön, the special iconic character, which basically distinguishes images and statues

from language and narration, takes center stage. In the image,
there is concentration on a fertile moment. In contrast, an action
process is presented in a narration. The genesis of an event or
an action cannot be represented with images. Action is com-
pressed in images; it is implicit, not explicit as it is in narration.
The image refers to something that can only be represented
iconically and not narratively, which remains implicit. An interpretation is only possible with the help of language. The image
"does not reveal" what it may look like; interpretations have only
limited significance for perception and sensual understanding of
the image.

An example: images initiate actions, i.e., can be performative
and have an implicit knowledge of an action that is represented,
showing, for example, a schematic drawing in an instruction
manual for the assembly of the cabinet. Although it only shows
one part of the assembly—how to join the walls of a cabinet—
the drawing is much more useful than a linguistic description.
The visual representation contains knowledge in a condensed
format that is not explicit from a linguistic viewpoint, and is as
an instruction more effective than an elaborated text. The iconic
character of the visual representation has implicit knowledge that
is helpful for the assembly of the cabinet.

If the world increasingly becomes an image, and image-producing
media start at an early stage to shape the imaginary world of
children and young people, then the image becomes a central
living condition. This is the case especially with the use of smartphones, apps, and computers, whose digital image-worlds are
incorporated through daily use, i.e., they become part of our
physical existence. We are already familiar with many things
as images before we encounter them, and then, when we do
see them, we have no means of knowing to what extent the
image seen earlier defines our encounter with the real thing.
If Comenius spoke about the insatiable thirst of young people
for images, then today the problem is increasingly how we can
protect ourselves from the plethora of pictures, how we develop

the skill to perceive images consciously as images, and how we incorporate and process them in their iconic character with their silent knowledge.

Performativity: Production and Performance

Initially, many research approaches to the iconic adopted a hermeneutical method, but in recent years, interest in the performativity of images and media has increased. This happened under the influence of the development of a performative perspective in the cultural sciences. In contrast to the hermeneutical approach, in which social practices are read as text and the interpretation of their significance is foregrounded, now, it is about how to envisage and examine the production and performance of the cultural and social. The iconic approach should thereby be complemented with a perspective that is present as implicit knowledge therein, but which did not play a role in the traditional interpretation of the social aspect. The perspective that had been implicit in this approach and therefore belonged to silent knowledge should now be discovered and developed. Now, it is no longer primarily about researching the significance and meaning of social and pedagogical actions, but about examining how these practices are executed. It then becomes clear that this perspective deals with practical knowledge, whose focus is on dealing with practices, with physical and social skills.

This is particularly apparent in the research of the "Berlin Ritual and Gesture Study" (Wulf et al. 2001, 2004, 2007, 2010 and 2011), which examines how people perform rituals, how they produce them, and how the ritual act differs in several performances of the same production. In contrast to Clifford Geertz, who understands culture as a "montage of texts" (Geertz 1995, 253), here the focus is on the actual act, its physical production and performance, as well as its productive design and layout (Wulf, Göhlich, and Zirfas 2001).

The perspective of the performative aims not to replace the
hermeneutical interpretation of the social element, but to
complement it by shifting the viewpoint. It is less about the
interpretation of the significance of practices than about the
production and performance of the act, its physicality, and its
interactions. The focus is not on an acceptance of a demanding
interpretation of social practices, but an analysis of the concrete
conditions of the act. It is "less about underlying issues than the
phenomenal event, less about the structure and the functions
than the process, less about the text or symbol than the creation
of reality" (Wulf and Zirfas 2007, 10). The emphasis is on interaction processes and the dynamics of linguistic performances
and completed actions, as well as the physicality and materiality
of the social element.

The objective is to research the modus operandi, the manner,
the way in which social practices are executed. Insofar as it
relates to a skill, according to Ryle (1990), this is embedded in
the silent knowledge of the body. Their institutional and his-
torical-social conditions play an important role here. To examine
these connections using a conclusive method, ethnographic
research is required. Here it is necessary to examine the social
situation in different ways: first, from the perspective of one or
several observers not involved in the event in a participatory or
video-supported participatory observation, and second, from
the subjective perspective of the actors using interviews and
group discussions. Then both perspectives are interrelated and
integrated where possible. In this triangulation attempt, the
difference between knowledge from a third-person perspective
and knowledge from a first-person perspective is made clear.
In both forms of knowledge, there is theoretically non-tangible,
implicit practical knowledge.

Human Beings and Things: The Materiality of Educational and Learning Processes

The iconic turn led to the examination of the significance of images, immaterial aspects, and digital media for society and culture. An anthropological interest in the diversity of images, the complexity of imagination, and the social and cultural power of the imaginary evolved. At the same time, it became clear how central this area is for individual and social activities and what role these images play in desire, in feelings, and in actions. In the interest of research on performativity, the significance of the body, which has been the focus of anthropology since the 1980s, was presented. Physical dynamics in social activities, which had been overlooked for a long time, were examined. The production and performance of senses and the body, and the performativity of social practices received attention. The performativity of images and media was discovered: a new interest developed in the materiality of human interactions, as well as things and their socializing effects.

Two developments supported this focus on the material element. One led to a discovery of the importance of technical equipment and prostheses for the body and the human conception of itself. Donna Haraway's idea of a "cyborg," a "hybrid of machine and organism" (Haraway 1995, 33), became a reflection of this fusion, which generated numerous figures and narrations in science fiction. Another development was the actor-network theory (Latour 2000), which clarified that not only subjects played a role in social activities, as was long suggested by the agency dis-course, but that social activities are effected by a range of factors in which the materiality of things plays an important role. The aim of this theory is to deal with the dichotomy between human being and thing, nature and human being, subject and object, and to reduce this dichotomy where possible. The comparison of human being and thing was no longer appropriate; it was thwarted, and the way new perspectives might arise for the relationship

between human beings and the world was examined. In Bruno
Latour's "symmetrical anthropology" an attempt is made to
overcome the sharp distinction between human being and thing.
The links between humans and things are analyzed. Things are
understood as being a result of human productivity and as a
consolidation of cultural development. When dealing with things,
complex historical processes may be experienced in a condensed
form.

Today computers, tablets, cell phones, etc., are part of people.
Without them, everyday life in most parts of the world is virtually impossible. In the digital native generation, these devices
or their effects are incorporated from early childhood and are
thus part of everyday life. They are used to expand and intensify
contact with the world. These devices take on the burden of
memory and make it possible to store and share large quantities
of data. Apps facilitate orientation in the world and solutions to
everyday problems. SatNav relieves us of searching; it suggests
reliability and orientation. Without SatNav, we would be helpless
and disoriented. The symbiosis between machine and human
being is likely to reach new levels in the driverless cars of the
future. It relieves human beings of driving, but also increases our
dependency on machines. Machines are part of our activities,
our body, our imagination and world of ideas. For a long time
now, they have no longer been external, on the outside; they are
part of us, meaning a demarcation between them and human
individuals is barely possible.

Latour refers to the fact that "each thing that changes a given
situation, by making a difference, can be an actor" or an "actant"
(Latour 2007, 123). The result is that where human and non-
human agents are combined, original "action programmes"
(Latour 2000, 216) are changed; new social practices thus evolve
such as people meeting up at extremely short notice via cell
phones. Many new action programmes can substitute a human
actor with a thing; answering machines are a good example. In
addition to this "delegation" (Latour 2000, 227), Latour also makes

reference to the fact that nobody is aware of the character that is made up of many such hybrid actors ("blackboxing," ibid., 227), meaning there is a "need for an unbiased, rigorous reconstruction of the historically developed links between people and things" (Nohl and Wulf 2013, 6). To research these links, historical and empirical studies of the materiality and the handling of the artifacts are required. In addition, historical analyses and ethnographical research are required.

In the humanities, there is a reception of the confrontation not only with the materiality of the human body and social practices, but also with the materiality of things (Nohl and Wulf 2013). Mimetic processes play an important role in these forms of cultural learning. Using the example of Walter Benjamin's "Berlin Childhood around 1900" and its reconstruction of childhood (Benjamin 1980), it becomes clear how the world of his parents' home is revealed to the young Benjamin in mimetic processes. In these processes, he incorporates the materiality of the spaces, rooms, streets, houses, and things. He shows how the rooms and things initiate feelings, how his world as a child is magically set up, how he imitates a windmill with his body, and thus experiences the machine character through his own body. In corners, hidden spots, dens, bays, cupboards, dressers, sills, etc., Benjamin feels the world of things; he has tactile experiences, and absorbs odors, which are incorporated in mimetic movement (Gebauer and Wulf 1998). The things are not lifeless. They look back, they make sounds, they smell, and convey tactile experiences. In mimetic processes, the objects and noises from early childhood are collected in the "deeper self," from where they can be recalled later by means of optical or acoustic stimuli. In the act of remembering, there is a mimetic reference to the things, the material of the memory. The mimetic ability of the child to relate to the objects of the world, to create something similar, to read them, returns to language and writing according to Benjamin's view. In the process the "mimetic ability," which was previously the "basis of the vision," creates in language and writing the "complete archive of nonsensuous similarity." The similarity and resemblance create central constellations through which the relationship with things and itself gradually forms. The processes described here belong to a large extent to the area of silent knowledge, of which we only have a rudimentary awareness.

The materiality of things has a demanding character. Many social and cultural products are manufactured and arranged so that they lure children into engaging with them and handling them in a certain way. Often a social or economic staging or production underlies the way these products appear. Things are also staged in the area of pedagogy. In *Emile* from 1762, Rousseau talks about pedagogy from things. The things are to ask children to handle them in a certain manner. Their demanding character "opposes the free availability of functional objects by that alone, through which the subject is disposed, because the request pre-empts him" (Stieve 2013, 92). No more or no less do the things themselves request an understanding of a cultural order, as their meaning and relevance can be read from them immediately. "The purpose only dominates in the everyday, brief or fleeting use of things and the thing is overlooked … in favor of a function being implemented" (Selle and Boehe 1986, 11). Many contributions from early childhood and research on childhood demonstrate how objects initiate and control learning processes. Today, things are also having effects on people, in particular in and beyond the digital world. As they take on the form of images here, they may also appear—free of their materiality—in completely new combinations, possible only in the digital medium. A new world of things in the form of images emerges and leads to the development of iconic materiality in people's imagination. The processes implemented here also create new forms of iconic knowledge of the body, which becomes part of the everyday living environment of people.

Outlook

With the focus on unknowing and silent knowledge, a research field for the cultural sciences is proposed in which important results from the "turns" of recent years can be merged. In this connection, an extension and enhancement of practical and performative-related perspectives is required, and a willingness to develop new methods of access and forms of experience and reflection for dealing with practice in collaboration with digital media. Researching social practices and the implicit silent knowledge therein from the perspectives of the actor-network theory, imagination, performativity, and iconic materiality in the virtual world is a challenge from a conceptual and methodological viewpoint.

References

Adorno, Theodor W. 1978. *Minima Moralia: Reflections on a Damaged Life*. Translated by E.F.N. Jepcott. London: Verso.

Baudrillard, Jean. 1981. *Simulacre et simulation*. Paris: Editions Galilée.

Benjamin, Walter. 1980. *Berliner Kindheit um Neunzehnhundert: Gesammelte Schriften*, edited by Rolf Tiedemann und Hermann Schweppenhäuser, Volume 4.1, 23–304; Volume 7.1, 385ff. (final version). Frankfurt am Main: Suhrkamp.

Derrida, Jacques. 1972. *Die Schrift und die Differenz*. Frankfurt am Main: Suhrkamp.

Gebauer, Gunter, and Christoph Wulf. 1998. *Spiel – Ritual – Geste: Mimetisches Handeln in der sozialen Welt*. Reinbek: Rowohlt.

Geertz, Clifford. 1995. *Dichte Beschreibung: Beiträge zum Verstehen kultureller Systeme*. Frankfurt am Main: Suhrkamp.

Haraway, Donna. 1995. "Ein Manifest für Cyborgs." In *Die Neuerfindung der Natur*, edited by Donna Haraway, 33–72. Frankfurt am Main/New York: Campus.

Huschka, Sabine. 2017. "Bewegung." In *Schweigendes Wissen*, edited by Anja Kraus, Jürgen Budde, Maud Hietzge, and Christoph Wulf, 625–638. Weinheim: BeltzJuventa.

Kontopodis, Michael, Christos Varvantaki, and Christoph Wulf, eds. 2017. *Global Youth in Digital Trajectories*. London/New York/New Delhi: Routledge.

Kraus, Anja, Jürgen Budde, Maud Hietzge and Christoph Wulf, eds. 2017. *Schweigendes Wissen*. Weinheim: BeltzJuventa.

Kuhn, Thomas S. 1962. *The Structure of Scientific Revolutions*. Chicago: University of Chicago Press.

Latour, Bruno. 2000. *Die Hoffnung der Pandora: Untersuchungen zur Wirklichkeit der Wissenschaft*. Frankfurt am Main: Suhrkamp.

Latour, Bruno. 2007. *Eine neue Soziologie für eine neue Gesellschaft*. Frankfurt am
   Main: Suhrkamp.

Lyotard, Jean-François. 1979. *La condition postmoderne. Rapport sur le savoir*. Paris:
   Éditions du Minuit.

McLuhan, Marshall. 1964. *Understanding Media: The Extensions of Man*. New York:
   McGraw-Hill.

Nohl, Arnd-Michael, and Christoph Wulf, eds. 2013. *Mensch und Ding: Die Materialität
   pädagogischer Prozesse*. Sonderheft der Zeitschrift für Erziehungswissenschaft
   25. Wiesbaden: Springer VS.

Polanyi, Michael. 1969. "The Logic of Tacit Interference" (first edition 1966). In idem.
   Knowing and Being, Essays by Michael Polanyi, edited by Marjorie Grene, 138–158.
   Chicago: University of Chicago Press.

Polanyi, Michael. 1974. *Personal Knowledge: Towards a Post-Critical Philosophy. A
   Chemist and Philosopher Attempts to Bridge the Gap Between Fact and Value, Science
   and Humanity*. Chicago: The University of Chicago Press.

Polanyi, Michael. 1977. "The Body-Mind Relation" (first edition 1969). In idem. *Society,
   Economics & Philosophy: Selected Papers*, edited by R. T. Allen, 313–328. New
   Brunswick, NJ: Transaction Publisher.

Ryle, Gilbert. 1990. "Knowing how and knowing that." In idem. *Collected Papers*.
   Volume 2, 212–225. Bristol: Thoemmes.

Selle, Gert, and Jutta Boehe. 1986. *Leben mit den schönen Dingen: Anpassung und
   Eigensinn im Alltag des Wohnens*. Reinbek: Rowohlt.

Stieve, Claus. 2013. "Differenzen früher Bildung in der Begegnung mit den Dingen:
   Am Beispiel des Wohnens und seiner Repräsentation im Kindergarten." In
   Mensch und Ding: Die Materialität pädagogischer Prozesse. Sonderheft der Zeitschrift für Erziehungswissenschaft 25, edited by Arnd-Michael Nohl and Christoph Wulf, 189–202. Wiesbaden: Springer VS.

Virilio, Paul. 1996. *Fluchtgeschwindigkeit*. München: Hanser.

Wulf, Christoph, Birgit Althans, Kathrin Audehm, Constanze Bausch et al. 2001. *Das
   Soziale als Ritual: Zur performativen Bildung von Gemeinschaften*. Opladen: Leske
   and Budrich.

Wulf, Christoph, Michael Göhlich, and Jörg Zirfas, eds. 2001. *Grundlagen des Performativen: Eine Einführung in die Zusammenhänge von Sprache, Macht und Handeln*.
   Weinheim: Juventa.

Wulf, Christoph, Birgit Althans, Kathrin Audehm, Constanze Bausch et al. 2004.
   Bildung im Ritual: Schule, Familie, Jugend, Medien. Wiesbaden: Verlag für
   Sozialwissenschaften.

Wulf, Christoph, Birgit Althans, Gerald Blaschke, Nino Ferrin et al. 2007. *Lernkulturen
   im Umbruch: Rituelle Praktiken in Schule, Medien, Familie und Jugend*. Wiesbaden:
   Verlag für Sozialwissenschaften.

Wulf, Christoph, and Jörg Zirfas, eds. 2007. *Pädagogik des Performativen: Theorien,
   Methoden, Perspektiven*. Weinheim: Beltz.

Wulf, Christoph, Birgit Althans, Kathrin Audehm, Constanze Bausch et al. 2010.
   Ritual and Identity. London: Tufnell Press.

140   Wulf, Christoph, Birgit Althans, Kathrin Audehm, Gerald Blaschke et al. 2011. *Die Geste in Erziehung, Bildung und Sozialisation: Ethnographische Fallstudien.* Wiesbaden: Verlag für Sozialwissenschaften.

Wulf, Christoph. 2013. *Anthropology: A Continental Perspective.* Chicago: The University of Chicago Press.

Wulf, Christoph. 2014. *Bilder des Menschen: Imaginäre und performative Grundlagen der Kultur.* Bielefeld: transcript.

DATA

DATA BROKERS

SILICON VALLEY

DATA ANALYSIS

ETHNOGRAPHY

DISCOURSE MAPPING

On Knowing Too Much: Technologists' Discourses Around Online Anonymity

Paula Bialski

This chapter focuses on the way technologists approach the data they collect, manage, and analyze; at times feeling they can know too much and see too much about individual users, at times feeling that they know too little, leaving them hungry for gathering more data. Based on preliminary research in San Francisco among data brokers, hackers, activists, privacy teams at large corporations, app developers, bloggers, and cryptographers, I create a typology of characters that handle data. Using the metaphor of weaving, I imagine data as threads that make up a fabric. Using this metaphor, I ask: Who collects these threads? Who gathers them, weaves them, and who cuts them? How are data gathered and treated?

Introduction

There are moments in life when we overhear conversations we do not particularly want to hear. I was sitting on the late train coming home from Lüneburg to Hamburg—with nobody in the train car other than myself, my partner, who was asleep, and two Polish thugs in their thirties. Speaking in Polish, thinking nobody would overhear them, they started discussing, at normal volume, a drug heist they were planning in which they wanted to transport five kilograms of a drug to Sweden by ship using a smuggler. Using my keen understanding of Polish, I started collecting items of information: five kilograms, a boat to Sweden, thousands of euros, endless questions about how to find a smuggler that looked right, that police would not expect, how to not get caught. She should be a small chick. Or a fag. Or a couple. Who would do it? Who could they take advantage of? Even before their sexist and homophobic remarks, I thought to myself, "This has gone too far. I know too much." The train was nearing Hamburg, and I froze, thinking, "What to do now with all this knowledge?" A huge part of me wanted to track them with my iPhone—snap a few photos, record their conversation, and email the information to the Hamburg police, citizen's arrest style. Another part of me didn't want to track and trace them. Why should I be the one with the power to reveal who they were, just because I had this information? Their lack of knowledge of my surveillance of them deemed my tracking practices unjust. Should I strip these two of their intentions and freedoms to disassociate from this drug deal? My partner woke up, and after I told him what was happening, he started getting angry. These guys were being sexist? His chest puffed up, he turned around and started glaring at them. They barely noticed. The train stopped at Hamburg's central station and he stepped out of the train behind them. They still didn't notice. While the story ended with the two thugs leaving the station unaware of our existence, I still couldn't help thinking— what do people do when they really know too much, and what are the affective dimensions among people who know too much?

Each and every person has a particular form or pattern of life. As Gregoire Chamayou explained in *Drone Theory*, our daily actions are repetitive, and our behavior has certain regularities. "For example, you rise at roughly the same hour and regularly make the same journey to work or elsewhere. You frequently meet up with the same friends in the same places. If you are placed under surveillance, it is possible to record all your movements and establish a spatiotemporal map of all your usual doings. Furthermore, by intercepting your telephone calls, observers can superimpose your social network upon this map, determine which are your personal links, and calculate the importance of each one in your life" (Chamayou 2015, 75). As an American army manual explains: "While the enemy moves from point to point, surveillance tracks and notes every location and person visited. Connections between those sites and persons to the target are built, and nodes in the enemy's network emerge" (Chamayou 2015, 76).

These practices, behaviors, daily patterns of doing things are all identifying markers of who we are. Today's digital infrastructures of collection, transmission, analysis, and presentation have made continuous data-mining possible (Couldry and Powell 2014)—continuous mining of what makes up "us." As one of the technologists I met during my fieldwork in San Francisco explained to me, "You would be surprised how unique you really are. All this stuff about us being the same is all wrong when it comes to a data perspective." It is very easy to find that one particular 30-year-old man, born on April 16, who is exactly six meters tall and goes to work at eight in the morning.

Many everyday activities now produce data without requiring human meaning or construction (or even basic consent). Along with the innovation of sensor networks, individuals started producing not "'content' composed of messages containing intrinsic or constructed meaning, but mere data—temperature readings, status updates, location coordinates, tracks, traces and check-ins" (Couldry and Powell 2014, 3). Not one of these individual data types is necessarily meaningful in itself—but taken together, either through aggregation, correlation, or calculation, such data provide large amounts of information. "We are living through a transformation of governance—both its mechanisms and reference-points—which is likely to have profound implications for practical processes of government and everyday understandings of the social world" (Couldry and Powell 2014, 1).

To tackle this issue, Couldry and Powell explained that emerging cultures of data collection deserve to be examined in a way that foregrounds the agency and reflexivity of individual actors as well as the variable ways in which power and participation are constructed and enacted. While I agree with this statement in that it calls to re-evaluate tensions between structure and agency, plus control and resistance of the actor within our data-driven environment, the "actor" or "data subject" often points inquiry more towards the "user" and less at what is happening behind the screen, within the bodies and minds of the technologists who gather, operate and analyze our data. When Beer (2009, 999) noted that sociology must also "focus ... on those who engage with the software in their everyday lives," I would add that sociology must also focus on the way in which software engineers, system admins, and data analysts also envision the everyday lives of users—thus creating a more open inquiry into what types of decision are made, what types of battle are played out, and what obstacles exist in implementing technology that influences our everyday lives. As I will explore in this paper, technologists think about the data they collect, manage, and analyze—at times feeling they can know too much and see too much, at times feeling that they know too little, leaving them hungry for more.

These technologists operating drones or the analysts in San Francisco are the ones who see our patterns of life. Understanding their bird's eye view of us helps us think about their agency, which is in itself "fundamental to thinking about the distribution of data power" (Kennedy et al. 2015, 2). In order to think

through these two dimensions—agency and data power—my
research focuses on one key problem today: anonymity.

Bachmann et al. (2014), drawing from Strathern's "Cutting the
Network" (1996), have suggested that if you want to understand anonymity, you have to start conceptualizing it as the act
of making cuts in identifying markers. To engage in a form of
anonymity—such as facelessness, namelessness, or pseudonymity—means that one "cuts" these potentially identifying markers
of individuality and difference from a person. "Genuine gains and
losses of anonymity occur when a second party links, or fails to
link, personal information with the person to whom it belongs"
(Ponnesse 2013, 344).

This process of linking and de-linking is, according to Ponnesse,
"the result of a specific exercise of control" (2013, 344). Because
contemporary societies are increasingly based on networked
information and infrastructures, we are facing new questions
of how networks of information, properties, and people can be
linked or de-linked in order to produce, maintain, abandon or
modify anonymity—and who holds that control.

These cuts are today assisted or fully brokered by
specific technologies, or specific persons. When these cuts
happen—preventing one piece of information from reaching
another party (be it a person or server)—anonymity is being
played out. A cut could be made by side A of the anonymous
interaction, side B of the anonymous interaction, or both, but it
is also increasingly other actors who are influencing this cutting
moment: for example, system admins, privacy teams, and
data analysts. So rather than focusing on the way in which the
"user" makes cuts in potentially identifying markers of their own
individuality and difference, and rather than focusing on how
the "user" creates situational, relational, and partial forms of
un-knowability, invisibility, and un-trackability—I wish to focus
on people like the drone operator in Chamayou's story, or the
technologist I interviewed in San Francisco. For a number of

complex reasons relating to both the material structure and the socio-economic system within which the technologist operates, they are at times a powerful, and at times a powerless, mediating agent in how forms of anonymity become transformed. Moreover, the "technologist" is not just one person—each has their own different agenda. My interest in understanding them—and not the user—also stems from understanding and unpacking the "black box" (Star 1992) of how they often gather and know our "patterns of life," unbeknownst to us.

In order to explore these characters, and how they come to "know too much," I will do a few things in this paper:

Firstly, I will introduce the method in my work, which creates a typology of "characters who know too much." These are the data scientists, technologists, system admins, cryptographers, and app developers who come from various fields and dimensions of the tech industry. Some work for large corporations, some are creating their own start-ups. The reason I create these Weberian ideal types is not only to synthesize and explain the various characters and ideologies of the people who "know too much," but also to camouflage the identity of the subjects I interviewed—focusing less on the person and their identifying markers, and more on their affective dimension of handling data. I realize the methods of anonymizing data while doing a project on anonymity calls for much more explanation, but I will reserve that for another paper, and for the sake of time not take it up here.

Secondly, in order to unpack the actions of these figures who "know too much," I will work with this metaphor of "cutting" and liken data collection to textile production. This approach is inspired by the likes of Donna Haraway with her metaphors of yarn and culture, and more specifically, Janis Jefferies. Jefferies is a British artist and theorist who uses the metaphor of textiles to produce new knowledge around computing and digital technology. She suggests we focus on a material knowledge afforded by textiles, and pattern specifically, where surfaces of patterning make visible what was once invisible—the conceptual, emotional, textured (Jefferies 2012). In that vein, I imagine data as threads that make up a fabric. Using this metaphor, I ask: Who collects these threads? Who gathers them, weaves them, and who cuts them? How are data gathered and treated? What types of scissors make these cuts? Are they sharp, do they make clean, indiscernable cuts, or are they dull, leaving behind scars and shreds when cutting? Who is the seamstress or tailor that holds the scissors in this cut? Do some hold the scissors, but not make any cuts at all? Why is a cut made in the first place? These seamstresses and tailors have different agendas, and in this paper I will only begin my analysis of the techniques of cutting, showing you who the people are who know too much, and how they deal with what they know.

Introduction to Methods

The fieldwork for this study was conducted for a larger project titled "Reconfiguring Anonymity—Contemporary Forms of Reciprocity, Identifiability, and Accountability in Transformation." This three-year project, which began in August 2015, is a transdisciplinary endeavor bringing together social anthropologists, sociologists, media scientists, and artists to produce new insights into regimes of maintaining, modifying, or abandoning anonymity in contemporary, hybrid online-offline worlds.

I spent nearly two months in San Francisco in August 2015, and during this time I interviewed hackers, activists, privacy teams at large corporations, app developers, bloggers, and cryptographers. In total, I conducted 20 in-depth interviews that lasted from half an hour to a number of days. I also conducted one focus group with the privacy team of a browser provider, attended tech privacy meetups, and gave a public lecture (at the Wikimedia Foundation). This preliminary research then led me to participate in conferences and workshops for technologists, such as the "European Workshop for Trust and Identity" in Vienna in

December 2016, which brought together technologists working on various topics of transorganizational trust and identity matters.

My interviews were unstructured, and I found my contacts mainly through "hanging out" and asking my interviewees who to talk to next. Our discussions would be mainly around the way in which these actors treat data and the user's personhood, and the tools being developed to help anonymize the user, as well as to help store and encrypt data. We also discussed the future for anonymity or pseudonymity on the net.

Based on this fieldwork, I began seeing conflicts and congruencies in the way in which these technologists or data brokers handled, exchanged, and ethically approached personal data. In this paper, I will limit my ideal types to three "Information Tailors": aggregators, allocators, and analysts. While this paper marks merely the beginning of my analysis, I think these first three "ideal types" can help us think through the distribution of data power and the agency and reflexivity of the technologist in knowing and un-knowing information linked to individual persons while handing data. Again, to help visualize this process, I will liken data collection to textile production.

The Information Tailors

The Aggregator

These agents collect, log, and store data from users. They are a human-machine hybrid. They can be a technical mechanism, like a data packet storage system, which, crudely speaking, collects data packets from any information transferred from one IP address and stores it on a server. Data aggregation is a central structure of the net. Data aggregators can be found all over the net, from Google and online dating websites to small apps. When it comes to knowing too much, data aggregators are the ones who gather and prepare the data—or to use the fabric metaphor—gather tens, thousands, millions, billions of threads to make yarn or string. A "thread" here is an Item of Information (IOI), and they are combed, separated, and directed towards one server, or data store, or another. While aggregators do not necessarily "know" too much, they collect and log a multitude of data in order to create more knowledge for the users and their platform and product developers.

As one of the data aggregators who was building his own app mentioned, "Humans are giving up their privacy in order to engage in all sorts of beneficial practices (e.g., quantified-self apps)," and as an app designer, he decides which exact data needs to be aggregated, based on the premise of the app (e.g., a running app would aggregate the user's running speed and frequency, their running route, etc.).

This app designer felt that the more data we aggregate, the better—explaining data as a helpful, global brain. He stated: "With any system, once you start recording it, it exists some- where. So the question is rather, do I trust the overall system to look out for my own interests? And if I don't, how hard am I willing to work to make sure it does? Humans who engage in various practices that they hope is kept private or anonymous should not think about *disengaging* from sharing this infor- mation, but must help optimize a central system that can act as a reputation system, but also must collect and protect its user data." Returning to our tailoring metaphor, this app designer was excited to see more data, do more with personal data, while at the same time expressing his general feeling that those giving up their data should trust people like him who thread their data and store it—promising users that he can be trusted to encrypt this data and store it in the right, secure place.

Yet not all data aggregators have the same vision, that "having and collecting more is better." In a lecture given by an operating system developer and system admin, trying to motivate his fellow technologists, he suggested they should "aggregate less" by "logging less." As a background for those are not familiar with logging—an essential part of data aggregation—this technologist explained: "Logs are produced by networked services," e.g., a system administrator must log for debugging and have an audit trail and usability studies (how a website gets used), which is useful for analytics. The data that's being logged cover many areas, but in particular, he said, "there are some details which are more identifiable that produce these patterns of information that can be used about someone, but maybe that won't be used by that person. So IP addresses, *who* logged into a machine, there are mail headers that get logged, there are cryptographic parameters that get logged, there is a whole bunch of different stuff that creates finger-printable trails in these data sets."

"Logging less" is part of the practice among system admins and information scientists called "data minimization." It is a theoretical approach that originated in the 1980s along with networked infrastructure and information sciences, and is now seemingly only promoted among "identity management" activists who make it their business to think through personal identity protection and data management. Information scientists Pfitzmann and Hansen explained that this approach "means that first of all, the possibility to collect personal data about others should be minimized. Next within the remaining possibilities, collecting personal data should be minimized. Finally, the length of time collected personal data is stored should be minimized" (Pfitzmann and Hansen 2010, 6).

One aggregator explained: "By default, not even intentionally, we collect data, if we do nothing the data gets stored. But who is allowed to store the data? Deleting is also a conscious decision. And there is also a responsibility issue—who is deciding to delete what? There is an awareness problem."

Speaking passionately, he said,

> I think it's worth thinking about this—people often don't make this simple realization: if somebody is trying to get data about somebody else, from you, there are lots of different

ways you can resist them getting that data from you. But the simplest way to resist is to not have that data. It's a super stupid thing to come to, but that is the easiest way to resist giving data away to someone else. Just don't have it.

While I do not have time here to explain all the variations of data aggregators, their ideology and agendas, the two I have mentioned show that both sparsely knitted and thickly woven threads of data are in play. The technologists I mentioned favored sparse threads of data out of fear that these threads will fall into the wrong hands. The app developer believed that thickly woven threads would be more useful in making better-quality garments and that trusting the tailor and his technologies will help users share more data, in turn allowing the technologists to know more about the user's patterns of life.

The Allocator

In the game of "knowing too much" about the subject, data allocators are the actors who allocate which threads go into which fabrics. Allocators are usually the privacy teams in companies—the intermediary between the data aggregators, collecting the threads, and the data analysts who weave the various threads together to make a given cloth. The agenda of the allocators is to protect users from "knowing too much" about what data the company collects. These allocators think about their company's user, the image of the company, how much can be "known," and how much should be "left unknown" to the public. Allocators not only make decisions about what to do with the threads being gathered, but about which threads, or items of information, to gather in the first place. During my fieldwork, I learned that various large companies have entire privacy teams that protect the data of users and that these privacy teams act as gatekeepers. Smaller apps, where money is still scarce and the teams are composed of three to five people rather than a few hundred, might not feature a very thorough information allocator. One person can act as an allocator, a designer, and a manager—having many other jobs—and the amount of effort invested in protecting these data is perhaps not as great as in a privacy team, where the team's sole responsibility is guarding data.

One data analyst I spoke to explained their data aggregation and data allocation team: "There is room for new tools but at the moment a lot of data is just aggregated and not used." The reason it is not being used? The privacy team doesn't allow them to use it. He explained that users must be led to think: "We trust the companies that are aggregating this data, that they won't do anything with it that's too sensitive or gives away our privacy." In this case, the privacy team has to make sure this trust is not breached—allocating only a small ration of data to use, not allowing the users to know too much about other users. We can imagine allocators as gatekeepers in the game of knowing and forgetting.

The Analyst

Much as the name suggests, the analyst analyzes information about a user. They do so for various reasons—in order to gauge the user's engagement in their product or in order to create a new product for their company. The analyst collects various pieces of thread, or items of information—made accessible to them by the allocator—creates the fabric, and assembles the garment. Analysts are at times overwhelmed with the amount of data they have and the amount of knowledge they have about a user. One analyst at a large social networking platform said, "I have more information than you can ever imagine. The amount of things I know about the users is insane. I might think 'Hey, I don't know if I should be tracking this,' but I see that we have to do it. This is something that I have problems with sometimes."

An analyst has access to the data allocators and they weave the threads of data in one way or another to create a certain cloth; here meaning a certain function of an app. This same analyst, who described himself as a hippie, also explained his moral dilemma: "This is the job you have, to help people make decisions. So the more data, the better. But sometimes we also say 'Why are we doing this? The less data, the better.'" This dilemma seemed to me to be a dilemma of data power and his feeling of control: on the one hand, he was hungry to know more about the user and create more features, and on the other, he felt he was invading the user's privacy.

Another analyst, when speaking about the critique of big data and surveillance, lamented that "full anonymity will not give us precise enough data." What he meant by this statement is that data security means often having less data, deleting it, or storing it securely. But in order to make systems faster, provide more features, and make these systems more usable, he has to have more data, and know more about users. This is the usability-data security tension. "How do we prioritize somebody's need for anonymity over the functionality of a system? Those who design and implement products that deal with the user's privacy often want to do their job well, and in order to do so, need to have the most data possible" (data analyst, San Francisco, August 2015).

This moral dilemma is not one that happens on an everyday basis for these technologists. As another analyst said, "Those who design and implement anonymous systems are just technologists, they aren't philosophers or sociologists, their decisions are not completely thought through—they don't consider all possible thoughts going through their heads. The efficiency of developing a product suffers from not having all eyes on everything. In extreme cases, the developer won't think of all of the problems (i.e., privacy or anonymity issues)."

This again creates an instability in the user's sense of anonymity, or what they think they revealed and what they think their receiving parties know about them. One data analyst I spoke to only collects information about a user's transport routes and cell phone provider. He explained that he often came into conflict with his privacy team because they did not allocate enough data for him to use. This constant linking and cutting of information is at work in the tension between what the analyst is allowed to know, what they are allowed to invent, what they want to know, and what they feel is personally crossing their moral boundary of "knowing too much."

Conclusion

This paper explores the first stages of analysis in an ongoing description of "people who know too much," in which I hope to unravel the stories of the anonymity tailors who make cuts or links in how anonymity is practiced online. I believe that to fully understand how anonymity is done today, and more generally how personal data are handled, qualitative research should investigate the nature of "cutting" data, the tools that are used to cut and link, and the ideologies and agendas for doing so. Further investigation around big data should also take into account the voices of the software engineers, system admins, and data analysts who affect—both directly and indirectly—the everyday lives of users. Doing so will reveal what types of decisions are made, what types of battles are played out, and what obstacles exist when handling personal data. This description of the affective dimensions of cutting and linking can hopefully further reveal how anonymity is being reconfigured, and explain the entangled weave of the technical and the social.

References

Bachmann, Goetz, Michi Knecht, Gertraud Koch, Nils Zurawski, and Ulf Wuggenig. 2014. "Reconfiguring Anonymity: Contemporary Forms of Reciprocity, Identifiability and Accountability in Transformation." In *Grant Application: Volkswagen Stiftung*. Accessed November 2016. http://reconfiguring-anonymity.net/blog/wp-content/uploads/2015/07/Project_description_web.pdf.

Beer, David. 2009. "Power through the Algorithm? Participatory Web Cultures and the Technological Unconscious." *New Media & Society* 11: 985–1002.

Chamayou, Gregoire. 2015. *Drone Theory*. New York: The New Press.

Couldry, Nick, and Allison Powell. 2014. "Big Data from the Bottom Up." *Big Data & Society* 1 (2), July–December: 1-5.

Jefferies, Janis. 2012. "Pattern, Patterning." In *Inventive Methods: The Happening of the Social*, edited by Celia Lury and Nina Wakeford, 125–136. New York: Routledge.

Kennedy, Helen, Thomas Poell, and José van Dijck. 2015. "Data and Agency." *Big Data & Society* 2 (2), July–December: 1-7.

Pfitzmann, Andreas, and Marit Hansen. 2010. "A Terminology for Talking about Privacy by Data Minimization: Anonymity, Unlinkability, Undetectability, Unobservability, Pseudonymity, and Identity Management." Accessed January 30, 2015. http://www.maroki.de/pub/dphistory/2010_Anon_Terminology_v0.34.pdf.

Ponnesse, Julie. 2013. "Navigating the Unknown: Towards a Positive Conception of Anonymity." *The Southern Journal of Philosophy* 51 (3): 320–344.

Star, Susan Leigh. 1992. "The Trojan Door: Organizations, Work, and the 'Open Black Box'". *Systems Practice* 5 (4): 395–410.

Strathern, Marilyn. 1996. "Cutting the Network." *The Journal of the Royal Anthropological Institute* 2 (3): 517–535.

Authors

Andreas Bernard is professor of cultural studies and speaker at the Centre for Digital Cultures, Leuphana University Lüneburg. Publications include *Lifted. A Cultural History of the Elevator.* New York 2014; *Komplizen des Erkennungsdienstes. Das Selbst in der digitalen Kultur.* Frankfurt am Main 2017.

Timon Beyes is professor of sociology of organization and culture at Leuphana University Lüneburg, Germany, and at Copenhagen Business School's Department of Management, Politics and Philosophy, Denmark.

Paula Bialski is a Junior Professor for Digital Sociality at Leuphana University. She is an ethnographer of new media in everyday life, looking at contexts of usage as well as production, and she frames her research within cultural, social, and media theory in general, and science and technology studies in particular. The goal of her current research project, titled "Programmer Worlds," is to investigate the way in which everyday practices of corporate software developers affect our digital infrastructures.

Matthias Koch is a research associate at the Institute for Advanced Study on Media Cultures of Computer Simulation (MECS) in Lüneburg, Germany. His research interests include the history and theory of media historiography, the history of science, phenomenology, and the works of Friedrich A. Kittler and Hans Blumenberg.

Martina Leeker is professor of methods in digital cultures and senior researcher at the Centre for Digital Cultures (CDC), Leuphana University Lüneburg. Her research interests include art and technology, critique in digital cultures, systems engineering and infrastructures, theater and media, and practical research.

Alexandre Monnin is a philosopher, research Director of Origens Media Lab, researcher at ESC Clermont and president of Adrastia association. He pioneered the philosophy of the Web and works on the Anthropocene and the end of digitality. Previously researcher at Inria and the architect of Lafayette Anticipations' digital platform, he has been an expert for the French open data agency since 2013.

Jeannie Moser is a postdoctoral fellow at the TU Berlin. She publishes on literature and science, the poetics and history of knowledge, and cultural studies. Her works include: *Psychotropen: Eine LSD-Biographie*. Paderborn 2013; Höcker, Arne, Jeannie Moser, and Philippe Weber, eds. *Wissen. Erzählen. Narrative der Humanwissenschaften*. Bielefeld 2006; Herrmann, Hans-Christian von, and Jeannie Moser, eds. *Lesen. Ein Handapparat*. Frankfurt am Main 2015.

Claus Pias is professor of history and epistemology of media, director of the Institute for Advanced Study on Media Cultures of Computer Simulation (MECS), Centre for Digital Cultures, and the Digital Cultures Research Lab at Leuphana University Lüneburg. His main areas of interest are media theory, the history of science of "media thinking", and the history and epistemology of simulation and cybernetics.

Christoph Wulf is professor emeritus of anthropology and philosophy of education and co-founder of the Interdisciplinary Center for Historical Anthropology at Freie Universität Berlin. His research interests and various publications focus on historical and educational anthropology, mimesis, intercultural education, performativity, and ritual.

www.ingramcontent.com/pod-product-compliance
Lightning Source LLC
LaVergne TN
LVHW092334060326
832902LV00008B/628